RUTHLESS

RUTHLESS

Scientology, My Son
David Miscavige, and Me

RON MISCAVIGE

WITH DAN KOON

St. Martin's Press
New York

www.stmartins.com

Cataloging-in-Publication Data is available from the Library of Congress.

ISBN 978-1-250-09693-7 (hardcover)
ISBN 978-1-250-09694-4 (e-book)

Our books may be purchased in bulk for promotional, educational, or business use. Please contact your local bookseller or the Macmillan Corporate and Premium Sales Department at 1-800-221-7945, extension 5442, or by e-mail at MacmillanSpecialMarkets@macmillan.com.

First Edition: May 2016

10 9 8 7 6 5 4 3 2 1

To my children, Ronnie, Denise, David and Lori;

my grandchildren and great-grandchildren,

some of whom I have never met;

as well as to the families that have been

torn apart by the policy of disconnection

as practiced by the Church of Scientology

CONTENTS

PROLOGUE

THE POCKET T-SHIRT IS A HANDY ITEM. CELL PHONES, READ-
ing glasses, shopping lists—they all fit neatly inside that little cloth
cavity. Of course, if you've got your cell phone in there and you bend
over, it will more than likely fly out.

In July 2013, I was living in Whitewater, Wisconsin, a town of
14,000 that lies 45 minutes southwest of Milwaukee. One morning, I
had to do some shopping at Aldi's market in nearby Janesville. I came
out with my bags and leaned in past the steering wheel to set them on
the floor in front of the passenger seat. As I did so, I reached up with my
right hand to keep my phone from falling out of my shirt pocket. I've
done that a million times. After you've dumped your cell phone or glasses
on the ground once or twice, it becomes an almost automatic action.

There is something called the butterfly effect. Mathematician and
meteorologist Edward Lorenz came up with the theory that a butterfly
flapping its wings in the Amazon jungle could result in a hurricane
some weeks later in the Caribbean.

Little did I know that the simple, automatic action of reaching my
hand to my chest was not only being observed but, like the butterfly's
wing, would set in motion events that I, and many others, never expected.

About a week later, I was sitting at home in Whitewater one evening when I heard a knock on the door. I answered and was surprised to see an officer from the Whitewater Police Department.

"Are you Ron Miscavige?" he asked.

I don't have a guilty conscience, but a police officer's appearance in a place where I have been living for only a few months and asking for me by name sent my antennae up immediately.

"Let's go to the garage so we can talk privately," I said.

I had no desire to alarm my mother-in-law unnecessarily. She did not have a clue about why my wife, Becky, and I had suddenly showed up in her life in the spring of 2012, and I was stumped as to what the officer wanted. I closed the front door, went around to the garage and opened it.

"What's this about?"

"I have some information for you," he began. "You have been followed by two private investigators hired by the Church of Scientology for the past year."

"What?! You've got to be kidding me!" Physically, this was like being punched in the gut. Emotionally, I was totally shocked.

"No, sir, I am not kidding about this."

"Jesus Christ, man. I'm being followed?" I could not believe what I was hearing. It was totally out of the blue.

"As far as getting more information about this, you can go to the West Allis police station because they are the ones that arrested one of the PIs."

The officer left, and I called Becky, who was at work, to tell her what had just happened. My mind was racing. I began scouring the past year of my life, trying to find clues. Who had been following me? Were there signs that I had ignored? I told myself I should have known something was going on. How could I have been so blind? After a few minutes of mental cacophony, my head cleared and I contacted the police in West Allis. They arranged for me to come down, but the very next day they sent someone over from the U.S. Bureau of Alcohol, Tobacco, Firearms and Explosives (ATF) with another member of the Whitewater police to check my car. Apparently, the PIs had attached a GPS device to my car to track my movements. I was even more stunned, if that was possible. Honestly, I was in disbelief about the whole thing. Life had been going really well, and suddenly a bombshell was dropped right in the middle of it.

The ATF agent wasn't feeling well, however, and he never completed the check of my car to locate the GPS, but the following day Becky and I went down to West Allis and talked to the police. They sat us down at a long table in a conference room. Shortly, the detective who had made the arrest a few days earlier came in and introduced himself as Nick Pye. He was built like an NFL linebacker who could bench-press 400 pounds, and, after we got to know him, it turned out that he actually could bench-press 400 pounds. Yet his demeanor was utterly calm and unpretentious. In my experience, those are the toughest guys of all—the ones who don't need to act tough.

"I am going to fill you in on what happened, but, first, let's get your car checked out," he said.

We brought the car into the service bay where they work on the police cars. They put it up on a lift and a mechanic checked the wheel wells.

"Yep, this is where they had one," he said, pointing up to a rear wheel well. "It's no longer there, but you can see the scratches where the magnet was," and he shined a flashlight up into the well so I could see the spot. I'd been driving around for a year broadcasting my every turn to the two guys that had been following me. Goddammit, what a sickening thought.

"This is wild," I said to Detective Pye. "I can't believe it."

"Do you have any idea why they were following you?"

"Well, maybe they were concerned that I would go to the media or something. I'm the father of the Chairman of the Board of the Church of Scientology, and last year we left the organization. And maybe he was a little concerned about my health. But I really don't know." I was fumbling for an answer because the whole thing was still unreal to me.

"Listen," he said, "I hate to tell you this, but I'm going to have to."

He thought for a minute, and I could see that he was searching for the right words. I was a little apprehensive. What now? Finally, he let me have it straight.

"Look, they saw you in a parking lot at a store, and you bent over and grabbed your chest with your hand. These two guys thought you were having a heart attack. Their instructions were to call if anything like this happened. When we pulled them in, they told us that none of the PIs had ever spoken to your son before. The routine was that they would contact the PI firm they were working for. The head of the PI firm would call an attorney, and the attorney would forward the information on to your son.

"So they called their contact, and within minutes a man who identified himself as David Miscavige called them and he told the PIs, 'If he dies, he dies. Don't intervene.'"

To say that I was shattered by Nick's words is the understatement of the century. Shocked, stunned, incredulous—fill in your own adjectives. I couldn't believe my ears. In fact, I heard it but did not accept it for quite some time. I think it is one of the most basic human impulses to help others, especially someone who is in dire need and *especially* a family member. And for a son to say that about his own father—just to let him die?!

This book is the story of how that came about.

ONE

BEGINNINGS

ON APRIL 30, 1960, A COOL, CRISP MORNING, I SAT IN THE waiting room at the Lower Bucks Hospital in Bristol, Pennsylvania. My wife, Loretta, was in the delivery room. Three years earlier, we'd had our first child, a son we named Ronnie. Now we were expecting twins. Loretta was a nurse, as was her sister Dolores, who was assisting in the delivery. I sat there waiting, waiting, waiting, growing more nervous by the hour. Suddenly, the doors burst open and the obstetrician, Dolores and another nurse came out. All three were holding blankets. Yikes, I thought, she had triplets. Well, the bright side was another tax deduction. We already knew she was going to have twins, so a third didn't bother me at all. I liked kids. I enjoyed having them around.

I sprung up and went over to Dolores, opened up the first blanket and looked into the blue eyes of my daughter, Denise. "Hi, little kid," I said and gave her a kiss. I went to the next blanket, pulled it back, and there was another set of baby blues looking back at me, David's. I gave him a kiss. The other nurse threw the third blanket up in the air and they all laughed. A little joke on the proud papa and the beginning of my relationship with my son David.

I know that life takes many twists and turns and that we can't hope to see what the future holds, but when I think back to that moment and my first look at that sweet little face, it's still hard to understand the transformation that took place.

My reason for writing this book is to focus on the journey David's life has taken. As a grown man, now middle-aged, he still possesses the energy and intelligence that I saw in him as a child. But, while he employed those traits in his youth to get excellent grades in school or to become good at hitting a baseball, today he sits atop a multibillion-dollar church that is controversial, litigious, secretive, manipulative, coercive and, in my mind, evil. Yes, I firmly believe that Scientology has morphed into an immoral organization that hides a long list of abuses behind First Amendment protections.

I was born and raised in the Pennsylvania coal region. There I learned a healthy respect for honesty and industrious work but also a commonsense attitude about rules, regulations and authority. By that I mean that I think the spirit of the law is more important than the letter. When Loretta and I started our family, we tried to pass on these same values to our kids. We had two boys and two girls: Ronnie, the twins Denise and David, and the youngest, Lori. Each learned the value of hard work, but I have come to realize that a parent can do only so much, and a child ultimately determines his or her own path.

For many years now David has been the head and ultimate authority of the worldwide Church of Scientology. He came into positions of power in the early 1980s and assumed full, uncontested control several years later after a power struggle with the two people that Scientology founder L. Ron Hubbard had allegedly appointed as his successors. In earlier years, David's accomplishments were a source of fatherly pride, but they no longer are because I came to learn and experience firsthand the mean streak and ruthless ways that surfaced after he left home and went to work for the organization.

L. Ron Hubbard was a writer by profession, and in 1950 he published *Dianetics: The Modern Science of Mental Health*, the book that evolved into Scientology a couple years later. Now, Hubbard was never all that the church has made him out to be. One can read church publications or one of its websites and come away with the impression that Hubbard was a demigod, a master of any activity he put his mind to, and humanity's greatest friend. The reality, as I have come to see, is somewhat different, which I will explore later. Yet I believe that if one reads a smattering of his writings or listens to even a few of his lectures, one cannot but conclude that, for all his personal shortcomings, Hubbard did possess a sincere desire to see people become happier, understand themselves better, improve their lives, and through that to improve society and the world.

Hubbard headed Scientology from its inception until his death in 1986, and so long as he was in charge, the focus of Scientology was to help people achieve those stated purposes through study of the philosophy he developed and to apply it in life as well as to one another through the counseling techniques he called auditing. Scientologists purchased Hubbard's books and lectures and paid fixed donations to receive auditing or to take courses to learn how to become an auditor and audit others. Delivering these services is how Scientology organizations obtained the wherewithal to continue to exist.

In David's regime this has changed diametrically. Today Scientologists are pressured to donate money to pay for a new building for the church in their city and then to donate more for renovations to convert it into a grand edifice. The coercion exerted by church staff on public Scientologists to cough up has wrought financial hardships on many people and their families. The Internet is full of such stories.

One Sacramento couple borrowed everything they could against their home equity when real estate prices were high; when the housing market crashed in 2008–2009, they were forced to declare bankruptcy. An owner of an insurance company donated upward of $10 million to Scientology; his company went bankrupt when the economy crashed in 2008. My own involvement with Scientology began in 1969, long before these arm-twisting practices began. In those years, I was a regular parishioner in the movement. In 1985, I went to work inside the organization itself, becoming what is termed a staff member, which is a different animal than regular public Scientologists. Because of that I was never subjected to the demands for money, which were not prevalent during my early days involvement with the subject. But I know my son, and I don't doubt the tales I read.

The Scientology movement under David's authoritarian leadership has morphed from a group that I believe was basically sincere in its efforts to help people understand themselves and better their lives to one that, today, I am sad to say, is primarily a coercive organization. I have watched this transformation over more than forty years. David runs Scientology with an iron fist and, to my mind, it has become a cult, pure and simple. I believe that his obsession with power and control have made him do things that will shock many, just as I was shocked when I learned that he had instructed the PIs following me to let me die.

On his watch, the church has spent millions to follow, harass and intimidate Scientologists, critics and former members who dared to leave the church and speak publicly about the abuses they suffered inside the organization as well as since leaving. Though the church under founder

L. Ron Hubbard took actions to silence critics long before David came to power, David has spent outrageous sums and gone to great lengths to carry on the practice. Any person the church perceives to be a threat or an enemy becomes fair game, and all manner of tactics, including litigation, private investigation and infiltration, are used to discredit or, better still, utterly ruin the target. The church denies that it does anything illegal or unethical and argues that it has been targeted by hostile government and private forces. But believe me, I know what I am talking about, far better than I wish I did.

To my mind, perhaps the most despicable acts the church engages in under David have been the destruction of family relationships owing to a policy called disconnection, which forbids any contact between a Scientologist and a family member or friend who might speak critically of the church or of David personally. I have no idea of the number of families that have been torn apart by disconnection, but I know at least one—my own. Yes, even I, the father of the leader of Scientology, have had my daughters and their children and grandchildren "disconnect" from me because I dared to leave the organization. In that sense, I guess you could say that Scientology is an equal opportunity abuser. When challenged about disconnection, though, the church reliably cloaks itself with protections afforded by the First Amendment.

Say what you will about Hubbard or Scientology through the years, but a Scientologist from the 1950s or '60s, '70s or even the '80s would not recognize the subject and its organizations today under David.

How did Scientology arrive in the place it finds itself today? And how did things get so screwed up that my own son had PIs following me around for more than a year? I will shed what light I can on that from the perspective of a father from a small mining town in Pennsylvania and, later, from a desert compound in southern California.

Interest in Scientology and its practices is intense and polarizing. Most people hate it or, at the least, are extremely skeptical; a dwindling number support it unconditionally. The church's PR machine claims millions of members throughout the world. If there are as many as 100,000 worldwide, I would be shocked. Despite its thirst for mainstream acceptance, Scientology has always been on the margins of society. From its earliest days, it tended to attract the sorts of people who were looking for a different path through life. Because of David's corrosive management style, any influence it manages to exert is negligible, and today even that is shrinking. The mountains of bad publicity keep potential new members away, and the constant demands for money disaffect existing Scientologists, who then become inactive or quit outright.

One of my purposes for writing this memoir is to furnish a context for David's life and bring some understanding to his actions since he came to power in the church. Because his mother is no longer living, I have the unique opportunity and, I feel, a duty to explain things, and I intend to give a glimpse into his early years that no one else can. Better minds than mine have wrestled with the nature/nurture question—that is, whether our personalities are inborn or develop based on our environment—and still it remains unanswered. I will add only this: for my whole life I have believed that, regardless of the hand we are dealt, each of us chooses how we play our cards.

To understand David, I think it will help to say a little about the influences that shaped his mother and me, and that takes us first to northeastern Pennsylvania.

TWO

LIFE IN THE COAL REGION

S PEEDY BUTELO, JAKE PUPKO AND I WERE STRUGGLING UP
the cinder bank that spilled out of the abandoned Sayre shaft on
the north side of town. The company burned coal to heat the mine in
winter and dumped the residue outside the coalhole. Over the years the
pile grew to about 300 yards high, and getting up it was like climbing
through sand. Making it harder that day in 1944 were the five gallons
of gasoline we were carrying after a fourth friend had lifted them from
another mining operation. We did not want the gas to go to waste and
had a plan to put it to good use.

Finally, we made it to the top of the plateau. Going down was a lot
easier and more fun than coming up because you could take a running
start and jump off the bank, and the loose cinders cushioned your land-
ing. We had other things in mind that day, however.

Scrounging around, we found some old tin cans, filled them with
the gas and doused the entrance to the mine. The hole was about six
feet by six feet, and we splashed the gas all around for a good 15 feet

inside. We saved a little and poured an igniter trail to the outside. We did the math and figured that 15 feet outside the hole was far enough to be safe.

I lit a match and held it to the trail. No dice—it didn't catch. We moved a little farther in and Speedy tried with another match. No luck.

Two steps closer, we tried again. Damn, nothing. The stupid trail of gasoline would not light.

Now we were about three feet from the entrance. Jake was suddenly overcome by bravado. "Screw this!" he said and grabbed the entire book of matches, lit it and chucked it into the hole.

KABOOM! It was like somebody flipped the switch on a 747. It blew out with such force that it burned off our eyebrows and singed our hair. We smelled like chickens that had been plucked with a blowtorch and were certain we had passed through the gates of hell.

Not only that, but the blast ignited the cinders and the mountain caught fire. We spent the rest of the afternoon stomping, beating branches and throwing dirt on the flames, anything we could do to get that fire out.

We were eight years old at the time.

Mount Carmel, where I was born in 1936, is a small mining town in northeast Pennsylvania. You pronounce it with the accent on *Car*, CARmel. State Route 61 runs through the center of town. The whole place is about one mile square with streets laid out in checkerboard fashion. When I was growing up, Mount Carmel had more than 17,000 people but has shrunk to only a third of that today.

I am reminded of something David said in the early 1980s when we were driving through town to a reunion of his mother's extended family. He turned to me and remarked, "You know, I wouldn't want to live in Mount Carmel."

"Why?" I asked.

"You couldn't affect the world very much from here."

This was before he had risen very high in the organization, and I suppose it was a harbinger while also an accurate assessment of Mount Carmel's place in the world.

The day of my birth, January 19, my dad tried to drive my mother to the hospital but his car got stuck in the snow, so he took her back inside the house. He called our family doctor, Dr. Allen, and he came down. But his car got stuck in the snow, too, so I was born at home.

I lived in Mount Carmel until I was 17, and, despite David's assessment many years later, I have to say it was a great place to grow up. In the 1930s and 1940s, the prevailing attitude to just about everything was laissez-faire. So long as you did not break the law *too much,* you were okay. You could bend it quite a bit, though. I have carried that attitude with me my whole life, and I am certain my children absorbed some of it.

People were hard workers and most worked in the coal mines. The town was like a little Europe. My family was Polish, but there were also Slovaks, Italians, Irish, Germans and others, truly a great potpourri of humanity.

Football was king. People lived and died by the fortunes of the high school team. If you were on the Mount Carmel football team, you could do no wrong. You could be caught robbing a store, and the cop would scold the storeowner for reporting you. (Criminals who didn't play football, however, did not have it so good. The cops were tough on anybody messing with the hardworking people of Mount Carmel.)

On Friday nights in the fall, the band and cheerleaders marched down Third Street from the high school to the stadium, and the town turned out to cheer them on and follow in behind. After the game, people would head to Mattucci's, a bar and restaurant, to relive the game with drinking buddies. Great times.

We were too poor to afford an actual football, so we stuffed rags into a sock, tied off the end and—presto!—we had a makeshift football. We kids played touch under the corner streetlights and relived the glories of the evening in our own way until our mothers called for us to come home.

Most of the homes in Mount Carmel were row houses, small but cozy and comfortable in a way. People did not know any other way to live. They were born in to it, and that was life. When people died, the funeral director came and the casket was laid out in the parlor so friends and relations could come to pay their last respects.

Back then, a miner could buy one of those houses for $2,000 or $3,000. A miner made around fifty bucks a week and could raise his family on that. During summers I sometimes made pocket money by picking huckleberries and selling them door to door for 35 cents a quart.

One summer, my childhood friend Joe Sarisky stole a case of dynamite, ten gallons of gasoline, blasting caps and fuse from a bootleg coalhole. When the big companies felt that a mine was played out and no longer financially worthwhile, they would simply abandon it. Then a couple of enterprising guys would come in and continue to work the hole, and they could make a decent living that way. One of these abandoned mine shafts was where Joe got the dynamite. Some other kids and I spent that summer blowing stuff up in the woods. My mother, had she known what I was up to, would have said, "Now, Ronnie, don't get hurt," but she probably wouldn't have stopped me.

There was a saloon across the street from our house, another to the left and a third in back. Three saloons just in sight of our house. I slept on the top floor, and in summer I could hear miners going down the street and bickering about something of no consequence. During summer it was so hot it was unbearable, and I had the windows wide open.

One evening my friend Eugene Stabinsky's father and another miner were going at it. The whole Stabinsky family had a habit of giving people lip and thinking they could get away with it. It wasn't working this time, though. "God damn you—!" I heard one miner yelling and then Stabinsky's father pleading, "Look, I'm a married man with three kids—" followed by *whap! whap! whap!* and then silence. Force overcoming reason. Then, a few moments later, "Hey, buddy, I'm sorry. I didn't mean to hurt you. C'mon, I'll buy you a beer," and they went back inside and kept drinking.

Nearly every block in town had a saloon, but there were nearly as many churches. The Irish had a church. So did the Slovaks. And the Italians. The Polish had two churches. Two factions of Poles had been unable to settle an argument, so, rather than have to look at one another on Sundays, they built separate churches.

One really great thing about the diversity in town was the fantastic variety of ethnic foods. For block parties, the women would get together and take pride in cooking up their national dishes for everyone to enjoy. I can still taste the homemade pierogies, babkas (a pie made from potatoes), soppressata (a dry Italian salami), lasagna, homemade doughnuts and my all-time favorite, pizzelles. These are light, anise-flavored wafers that I learned to bake and still do to this day. Taste one and you are hooked.

Next to football, the other thing that people in Mount Carmel respected was music. If a miner saw a kid who played an instrument being picked on, he'd say, "Hey, lay off the kid. He's a musician."

My father, Anthony, was a musician. He could play piano, accordion, saxophone and clarinet. He had a band that used to rehearse in our living room, and I would lie there in my "go carriage" (that's what we called a baby stroller in those days) and listen to the music. When I was 11, I told my dad I wanted to start playing an instrument.

"What do you want to play?" he asked me.

"I dunno, a trumpet, I guess," I replied, and that was how I started.

Music just sort of came to me. The first time I picked up a trumpet, I got a pretty decent tone out of it. If I heard a song once or twice, I could play it. I knew all the standards of the day, and by the time I was 13, I was playing gigs. One time Tommy Butkevicz and I went into the bar across the street from his house. Tommy played piano and I played my trumpet. Afterward, we went around and the miners gave us a dime or a quarter apiece, which doesn't sound like much until you realize that you could buy a new pair of jeans at Penney's for $1.50 in the mid-1940s. Nobody kicked us out or said anything, and that was my first gig.

My dad had an insurance brokerage, and in a back room he set up a little instrument repair shop. Students from the high school would bring in their instruments, mainly woodwinds, and he would fix them up. He always lost money on the deal but did it because he was a good-hearted guy.

Maybe it was because his own life had been rough. He was born in 1899; he was six years old when his father died, so my dad had to go to work in the mines to help his mother. In those days kids would lead the mules into the mine or help sort the coal from the rocks.

He tried a lot of different things to make money and eventually settled on selling insurance. Before that he had a soda company that went bust because people didn't return the bottles. Another time he had a gas station, and in the basement of our house he put in a big tank that held the gasoline. It was a half cellar that had windows and you could see in from the outside. One day a neighbor came over and said to my mother, "Helen, I don't mean to tell you your business, but your son Tony took off the gas cap and lit a match to see how much was left in the tank." There's the old saying "If your time is up, your time is up." Nobody on the block's time was up that day.

That was life in the coal region, the values I grew up with and what I wanted to instill in my own children. For three of the four, I think it has worked out pretty well.

When I graduated from high school, my father said, "If you go to college, study business," but I didn't want to study business. If anything, I wanted to study music. I'd had a job playing at a country club six nights a week, but I didn't know what I wanted to do with my life. In other words, I was ripe for the picking by the first person with a good pitch.

THREE

MUSIC AND THE MARINES

ONE DAY DOWN ON OAK STREET I RAN INTO A RECRUITER for the Marine Corps, and he started talking to me, telling me about the Marines. His pitch worked, and I decided I wanted to be a Marine. Joining the military was a common option for guys leaving high school in Mount Carmel. A lot of guys joined different branches, but I happened to bump into a Marine recruiter first.

I enlisted and went to Parris Island, South Carolina, for boot camp. My first night there I thought, This is the worst goddamned mistake I ever made in my life. If you have ever seen Stanley Kubrick's *Full Metal Jacket,* that is exactly what boot camp was like. All we recruits got our heads shaved and were issued our uniforms and gear. That first night everybody, and I mean everybody, got his head slammed against the metal bunk or punched in the gut by the drill instructor. We stood at attention with all our belongings in front of our bunks, and the DI went down the row screaming and slamming each one of us. I thought I was safe, but just as he passed me, he shoved my head against the bunk and I saw blue flashes. What a welcome.

When he was leaving he told us, "Listen, I'm going to come in here in the morning and I'm going to say, 'Platoon 420, hit the deck.' If you're not standing at attention in front of your bunk by the time I turn the light on, God help you."

The next morning my eyes were wide open, even though I'd always had a hard time getting up early. I jumped out of bed just as he was walking into the barracks. He turned the light on, and a kid named Beltz in the top bunk next to me was still sleeping. The DI reached under the upper bunk and pushed him up; he banged his head against the next bunk and woke up flying through the air. That was how we started. Boot camp was rough.

There is an attitude in the Marines that goes, "Every Marine is, first and foremost, a rifleman." No matter what else you did in the Marines, you had to be a rifleman. That started in boot camp, and when we had to qualify on the rifle range, I earned the top shot out of the hundreds of guys who qualified that week. We had to shoot an M1 Garand rifle from 100, 300 and 500 yards, into a 20-inch target. At 500 yards I could hit the bull's-eye at least eight out of ten times without a scope, just using the sight on the rifle.

The following week we had mess duty, and I didn't have to wash a single pot the entire week. In the Marines you got rewarded if you did well. On the other hand, if you failed, you got punished. One guy in our platoon didn't qualify on the rifle range. They made him march ten feet in back of the rest of the platoon with his pants on backward, his shirt on backward, his hat on backward and his boots on the wrong feet. He was referred to as a shitbird, and when he marched out of step the DI kicked him in the shins—*whap!*

Rewards and penalties, it is called, and L. Ron Hubbard said that these should exist in Scientology as well. If you did your job well, you were supposed to be rewarded, and if you did poorly you were meant to be punished, such as by being paid less. Under David, the rewards went out the window for Scientology staff members and only the penalties remained. During my last twelve years working for the organization, I never got a liberty, not a single day off. I was not the only one in that boat, either. In the Marines, though, the policy was properly applied.

Ten weeks after having my head slammed against the bunk, I graduated from boot camp and said to myself, "I can make myself do *anything*." I became a disciplined individual. I turned from a civilian into a Marine. From then on, if I had to do something, I could make myself do it. That's a characteristic you can't get anywhere else as far as I know, except maybe the 101st Airborne or the Navy Seals. "Once a Marine, always a Marine." There's truth in that statement, and I used what I learned in boot camp in raising my kids, minus the yelling and abuse. But I did instill accountability in them as well as a work ethic.

After boot camp, they sent me to Camp Lejeune, North Carolina, for advanced combat training. One week I was chosen "Marine of the Company." The reward was a weekend pass, so I went up to Pennsylvania.

As I was returning to base that Sunday, there was a violent snowstorm. All the buses were canceled. Planes were canceled. I got back 12 hours late. They restricted me to the barracks for two weeks. There was no excuse, no excuse for failure in the Marines. Rewards and penalties.

"You say you couldn't make it back? You're a failure. You're a shitbird." That was the attitude, so I spent the next two weeks in my barracks.

After a month of advanced combat training, I was transferred to Quantico, Virginia. I worked in battalion headquarters, and my duty was to file a report by noon each day with an accounting of who was present, who was missing, in sickbay, whatever. The last thing my superiors wanted to do after drinking all night in the clubs was to mess with these reports, so they were extremely happy when I was able to get them filed on time each day.

By 12:00 I was done with that duty, and I asked the sergeant major, "What do you want me to do now?"

"Do whatever you want, kid. Just keep doing your job," was his reply, which meant I had the rest of the day off.

I used the time to go down and see if I could get into the band because I really wanted to play music. I had an interview and audition with one of the band members, who told me, "You qualify, but our TO [table of organization] is full up."

That was kind of a disappointment for me, but I figured, What the hell, and gave up on getting in the band. I started working out in the gym and began dating a girl in Philadelphia named Loretta Gidaro.

Later on, I heard about a talent contest on the base, and I decided to go down and play my trumpet just for the hell of it. And I won the show! First prize was $12.50, which I cashed in at the PX, caught a train and went up to Philly for the weekend to visit Loretta.

I came back to work on Monday morning and was greeted by a scowling battalion adjutant.

"You traitor!" he screamed at me. "What the hell are you trying to do to us?"

"What do you mean, 'What am I trying to do?'" I had no idea what he was talking about.

"You know it. You had this whole thing planned all along!"

"Had *what* planned?"

"The commandant has ordered you into the band immediately!"

The base commandant was at the talent show and he heard me. He ordered me into the band!

I spent the last year and a half in the Quantico Marine band and studied music theory and harmony at the Naval School of Music, and for the rest of my life I've used what I learned.

FOUR

STARTING A FAMILY

THERE'S A CERTAIN WAY SOME PEOPLE, PARTICULARLY MEN, express their affection for a friend, a kind of feigned antagonism punctuated by insults, cursing and a punch to the shoulder.

Well, one day, Loretta and I were sitting in her childhood home down on Seventh Street in Mount Carmel. We had been dating for a while and were just hanging out at her place. Her uncles were there, playing cards in the dining room, and the racket coming out of that friendly card game was something to hear.

"I had good cards that last hand," roared one.

"The hell you did! You don't know a damn thing about cards," came the rejoinder. On and on it went.

The noise level was unbelievable. I thought the house was going to bust apart at the seams. From where I sat in the living room, it sounded like an all-out fight was erupting. They weren't even mad at each other but were just being themselves, loudly, and that was the way they communicated. In fact, that is how I remember nearly all the Italians in my hometown communicating—very loud with lots of emotion and gesticulating.

I knew Loretta from high school. She was in my class but in those days was going with another guy, Joe Chango, who was the quarterback on the football team. Loretta was a cheerleader, and they made quite a couple. I had always found her attractive. She was about 5'2" and had dark hair and blue eyes and an olive Italian complexion, which I liked. A blue-eyed Italian. Very unusual. We didn't have too much to do with one another in high school, even though I had designs on her. Fat chance I had then, since she was going with the star of the team. After graduation, though, she went to Philadelphia for nurse's training, and Joe married another girl. When I found that out, I made a move. Loretta and I began dating not long after I joined the Marines.

Like most Italian families, Loretta's was close and demonstrative.

She brought this characteristic to our relationship, and it affected how we got along. You could say that the signature trait of our entire relationship was that we argued. A lot. As in, all the time. Still, I found her attractive and she was smart, but there were things we did not see eye to eye about. She was not shy about letting me know it, either, with her piercing stare or equally sharp tongue. So, while we stayed together for nearly 30 years, it was not without a level of strife. I admit that I had my doubts that this relationship would last long term. The day before we got married I even said to her, "Loretta, do you really think we should get married? We argue constantly."

"Oh, yes, Ron, we should. It'll get better after we're married. You'll see."

Of course, it only got worse since we were together all the time. The truth about why we got married was that she was pregnant. That's the way things were back in the 1950s: if you got a girl pregnant, you took responsibility and married her. Abortions were illegal, and although it was possible to get them, they were really frowned upon. I had just gotten out of the Marines and found a job working for an insurance company. Loretta had finished nurse's training and was working in a hospital in Philly.

When we were married in February 1957, we had both just turned 21. Nobody ever found out Loretta was pregnant—not our families, nobody. After the wedding my dad asked me to come back to Mount Carmel and work in his insurance firm, so we got an apartment on Oak Street, and I went to work for my dad. On September 4, our first child was born, a son we named Ronnie after me.

In the end, though, things in Mount Carmel did not go well. I had a falling-out with my dad (that we later patched up), so we moved down to Levittown, Pennsylvania, with Loretta's parents in 1958. My father-in-law got me a job with Hydrocarbon Research, and we rented an apartment in Bristol right next to the New Jersey border. Shortly thereafter, I took another job selling cookware. I did really well right away. My income shot up, and we moved to Willingboro, New Jersey, about 20 miles east of Philadelphia.

Except for the arguments with Loretta, life was good. I really enjoyed Ronnie, and I was making enough money selling cookware that I could pay all my expenses for the month with one week of work, which left us with a lot of extra money.

My good income had a drawback, however, and this explains something about the problems Loretta and I had in the marriage. Loretta came from a well-ordered family background. Her people were the salt of the earth. Her father worked in the mines while she was growing up, and it was a steady, secure job. He was always home for dinner, and the family ate together every evening. The family routine was stable. They went to Mass every Sunday. That is the way she grew up, and she wanted to bring that into the family she was raising with me. Unfortunately, a salesman's hours can be unpredictable, especially since I was selling cookware and I often had to make calls in the evening when people were home. This was a real bone of contention with Loretta because her vision of a stable family life did not include a husband who was entrepreneurial. The truth is that we had quite different personalities. Loretta wanted to raise kids and have a stable family life. I was a risk-taker and interested in finding some answers to life. Now, some marriages might work with two opposite personalities like that. But both Loretta and I were strong-willed, and it just never worked out. My kids will tell you that they cannot ever recall a time when Loretta and I got along.

Still, having Ronnie and later the twins Denise and David in my life was wonderful. I loved looking into their blue eyes, holding their tiny hands, hearing them gurgle and laugh. It was great.

When the twins were about three months old, we had them christened. I rented the Mallard Inn, a restaurant off Route 38 in South Jersey. Carlo and Augusta Racine were their godparents and carried them into the ceremony. We catered a nice big dinner for the guests and everybody had a really good time.

Our family spent David's early years in Willingboro. It was a wonderful place to raise a family in the 1960s. Half a block from our house, you went through a gate in a cyclone fence to a park with football fields, baseball diamonds and a swimming pool. I taught all my kids to swim by the time they were three years old, and they could dive off the three-meter board by age four.

I bought a two-story, white-shingled house that had red shutters. Our one-car garage was attached to the house, and if the boys climbed out their bedroom window, which they often did, they would be standing on top of the garage. The kitchen had an island stove, and I stood the kids on chairs around it while I taught them how to cook breakfast and other dishes.

When David and Denise were toddlers, I decided to build a play area in the yard for them so they could be outside but safe from the street. My father and I went to a lumber supply for posts, fencing, hardware and anything else we needed. We spent the day sledge-hammering posts into the ground, making sure everything was vertical, nailing the cross braces to the posts, cutting the fence boards, nailing them up, and making and installing a gate. It was a job and a half, but we were quite pleased with the result. I brought Dave and Denise outside to show them their new play area. They both immediately walked over to the fence, climbed up and over and looked at us, smiling proudly from the other side. The humor of the situation was not lost on either my father or me, and at that point all we could do was laugh.

I taught Ronnie and David how to play football and baseball. When Dave was a little kid, he could not hit a baseball for the life of him. I could toss him a beach ball, and he could not hit it with a tennis racquet. When he was about eight I decided enough was enough.

"David, come on," I said. "We're going to teach you to hit once and for all."

He, Ronnie and I grabbed a bucket of balls, a bat, and gloves and marched down to the park.

I began lobbing him pitches. Whiff. Whiff. Whiff. Foul ball. Whiff. Grounder. Whiff, whiff, foul. It went on like this for some time. Ronnie played behind me and shagged the balls whenever David made contact. David never got discouraged and kept at it. Then, at one point, bingo! His hand-eye coordination kicked in. After that he could not miss. I moved farther back and stopped lobbing and started pitching. Line drive. Line drive. Hard grounder. Long fly. He hit nearly everything I threw him, and after that he could hit. In Little League he must have hit .600. You could not get the ball past him once he got the hang of it.

Both he and Ronnie played "pee-wee" league football. Ronnie was three years older and played in a higher division, but Dave, small as he was, played too. I had to put two-and-a-half-pound weights in his shorts pockets so he could make the minimum weight for his team. He was really small. Even today, he stands, at most, 5'4". Like me, David was skinny as a kid, but he was tough and scrappy. Both Ronnie and Dave did well, and their teams won championships. David played free safety, and he was a determined player. Nobody broke loose for a touchdown on him. The boys would come home after a game, and their uniforms would be filthy. Loretta was always good about scrubbing and washing them, and by the next game they looked brand new again. In our own ways, both Loretta and I were very engaged parents.

As often occurs with little brothers, David idolized his big brother. Both were good students, but Ronnie was more athletically gifted. Ronnie never gave David any reason to dislike him, and they got along great. In fact, I don't think Ronnie ever gave anybody reason to dislike him, and I have been told that, as adults, Ronnie and David couldn't be more different.

Like most households with energetic kids, ours was often boisterous. Ronnie and Dave would sit in a cardboard box at the top of the stairs with their football helmets on and slide down, crashing at the bottom. All my kids were given a lot of freedom so long as they did their chores and listened to their mother and me. Other than that, they were free to do pretty much as they pleased. All of them, however, were fastidiously neat about their possessions and the rooms they shared.

Our last child, Lori, was born in 1962, two years after David and Denise, and at that point our family was complete. Lori also had blue eyes and was blonde like the others, but her hair darkened and became more like Loretta's as Lori got older. My work continued to go well, and, despite the number of mouths to feed, we still had plenty of discretionary income.

Both Denise and Lori were dancers. Loretta or I drove them to their lessons, and they learned tap dancing, ballet, jazz, you name it. In Atlantic City was a place called Tony Grant's, and he held talent shows for kids called "Tony Grant's Stars of Tomorrow." Denise and Lori danced in the shows as a sister act. On stage they were like shadows of each other, they were so in sync. Both had great moves and natural rhythm.

The Jersey shore was only about an hour's drive east, and we often went there for summer vacation. We'd spend the day at the beach, come back to our rented house, clean up and go out for a fish dinner. Those were wonderful times.

All the kids were good-looking, bright and a real joy to be around. Many days I would come home from work at night, and if they were still up we'd sit around the table and they would yap at me. I let them talk about anything and everything. I never talked down to them. I talked to them as individuals, and I think they liked that. They could tell me anything or ask me anything. "What'd you do today, Dad?" I'd tell them about my day and then ask, "How about you, Denise? What did you do?" We would sit around just talking to one another.

There was a tradition in the coal region that when you had company, you sat around the kitchen table, not in the living room, and had a beer or a cup of coffee. One time Bernie Lyzak, who played sax in a polka band I was part of, came for a visit with his wife, and when they were leaving he told me, "Man, your kids are just like adults. They can carry on a conversation about anything."

One thing about my kids: I never made them feel wrong for telling me things. I never made them feel guilty for anything they did. I would talk to them and sort out how to deal with it. I might tell them they had to do the dishes for a week as a penalty if they did something wrong, but then when it was over, it was over. Consequently, they were pretty open with me. That was something I learned as a kid. When an adult got on me for something I did wrong I felt bad, so I decided never to do that to my kids.

One time when he was a youngster, David got in a spat with a neighbor kid and punctured holes in the kid's bicycle tires with a dart. The kid's mother came over and let me have it. I defended David and sent her away. Then I shut the door and asked David, "Did you do it?"

"Yeah," he confessed, "I did."

I made him do chores for a week as a penalty and that was that. I never let things like that fester. Once they confessed and they took their penalty, it was over. This was years before Scientology, and I later realized that I should have made David apologize to the kid and buy him new tires to square things.

Ronnie was always smart and very athletic. He was really fast. In pee-wee football, once he got into the open, he was gone.

Denise was also really fast, but what I recall best about her is that she was super helpful. She always wanted to help us around the house or help other people. She was affectionate and extremely loyal. She would do anything for her friends.

Lori also wanted to help out whenever she could. One time, we were laying tile and Ronnie, David and Denise were helping. Lori was too young to help, so she snuck off into the kitchen and made little sandwiches and lemonade for us. That was her contribution.

What their mother and I instilled in them was the idea that you had to earn your keep. You can't just live life and expect people to give you something for nothing. In a family, you do whatever you can to help support it. I explained it to them like this: "Listen, I have a job to support us, your mother cooks for you, you have a nice house to live in, everybody in the family has a job, so here's what your job is . . . ," and they accepted that that was the way it worked. By the ages of three or four or five, they understood how things worked and they agreed.

One day Ronnie said to me, "Dad, I want to learn how to ride a two-wheeler bike."

"Okay, I'll help you, but I'll tell you right now, you aren't going to stop until you can pedal that bike by yourself."

We went out on a hot summer day, and I'd push the bike, then let go and the bike would fall over or he'd fall off. We kept at it and kept at it, and when how to do it kicked in, he was beaming with pride that he'd learned how to ride a bike.

The next summer, he was out front and David said, "Ronnie, I want to learn how to ride a two-wheeler."

"Okay," Ronnie said, "I'll teach you but remember this: we're not going to stop until you learn how to ride, no matter what."

Ronnie and Dave were always close, but in the future their roles would reverse, with David delivering the stipulations of how things would be.

When I peered into the future, I saw my kids growing up happy and healthy, following whatever passions they had found, one day marrying and starting families of their own, and me becoming a grandfather who could dote on my grandkids. If you had told me then that one day my son David would effectively cut me off from my own daughters and their children and *their* children, I'd have laughed in your face. Today I'd be dining on crow because that is what has happened. The Church of Scientology actively tears families apart, separating parents from their children, turning children against their parents, all the while claiming that forced disconnection does not exist. I'm telling you that it does exist, and my family is just one of many that have been victimized.

FIVE

A MARRIAGE
MADE IN HELL

B ACK IN THE 1960S, YOU'D HAVE THOUGHT I WAS THE HAPPI-
est guy in the world. I wasn't, although that had nothing to do
with my four bright, happy children.

Contrary to Loretta's prediction about how the relationship would
improve after we were married, things only got worse. Honestly, it was
a house of horrors for me and for Loretta too. Arguments were a daily
occurrence. They became such a regular part of my life that when I look
back, they blur.

On some occasions, however, things went beyond words. Both Loretta and I were products of the Pennsylvania coal region of the 1940s
and 1950s. It was a blue-collar area with blue-collar mores. The upside
is that people were hardworking, for the most part honest and good
neighbors. The downside is that many were alcoholics, and domestic
disputes were often settled with violence. I remember being up in my

third-story bedroom as a kid and hearing a woman on the street below saying to her coal-miner boyfriend, "I love you, I love you," even as I could hear his fists punching her body.

It pains me to admit it now, and I regret ever doing it, but there were times when I punched Loretta. I never slapped or hit her in the face but, still, sometimes I did strike her. I might punch her in the arm or push her away when she was getting on me. She threw things at me—pots, pans, a pot of boiling coffee once. After a fight I would think, Jesus Christ, this is no way to live.

For the most part, though, we just fought with words. Loretta passed away several years ago, so she cannot provide her perspective. I can say only that I would bring up something and nearly always she would oppose it. I would say something like, "I'm going to clean out the garage this weekend." Her response would be, "Oh, no, you don't want to do that. I need you to do such-and-such," and it would escalate from there. I felt nagged because she would get on me about totally unrelated things. Our voices would rise, and I would become more and more up-set. Many, many times, too many to count, I wound up feeling utterly deflated. I would sink down in my chair with my head in my hands thinking, This is ruining my life. Why do I let this happen?

At those moments, the strangest thing would happen. Loretta would calm down, too, and say, "Here, Ron, let me make you a cup of coffee. Here's a piece of pie." It was as if she had won the argument. And she had, because many times I felt exhausted and defeated. We would be out in public, and she would just snap and start yelling at me, which was embarrassing as hell.

The default state of our marriage was strife. I do not bring that up to paint myself as the henpecked husband or a victim. Were Loretta still alive, she undoubtedly could fill in the other side of the story. Suffice it to say, it takes two to tango and we both contributed mightily.

It boils down to—and I think this occurs in many relationships—an inability to tolerate the way the other person is. One person is holding an attitude about the other of "I think you should be this way, I think you shouldn't be that way, I think you should do this, I think you shouldn't do that," a list of attributes that don't exist in the other person but should, in the other person's opinion. The second person holds a similar attitude about the first, and so they enter an arena of combativeness that has no reason to exist except for an unwillingness to tolerate the person who is right there. Yet, if one could overcome that unwillingness, one might find that those intolerable things in the other person might fade away. That is actually what happened in my marriage to Loretta in later years.

An important detail of a larger point of the story is that we did not hide these spats from the children. They were witness to them, and I know they were scared. Just as I was when my mother and father used to fight back in Mount Carmel. My mother might get on my father about something and he would erupt. He never struck her, but sometimes he picked up a dish towel to lash her with. They would be screaming at each other, and witnessing their fights was traumatic for me—I depended on my parents for survival. Today I regret that Loretta and I exposed our children to those fights. Anyone who has known our son David as an adult can recognize some of the elements from those battles: the volatile temper, the refusal to let go of things and the tendency to try to dominate through nullification. Yet who can say for certain whether these tendencies were part of David's makeup from birth or they were learned? Because none of my other children expresses these traits, I am inclined to think that they were latent in him from the beginning. While I believe that Loretta and I shaped the lives of our children to a degree, each of our children makes their own decisions. Ronnie, for instance, is the most considerate and thoughtful person you would ever want to meet; yet he was exposed to as many of our fights as the others—more even, because he is the oldest. I guess every child processes what happens in the home in their own way since they turn out so differently.

The truth, however, is that Loretta's antagonism was really directed only at me. She was great with the kids. She cooked their food and made sure they were dressed well for school. She demanded that they do well in class and get good grades. She was nice to the neighbors. She was a good cook and homemaker; her lasagna was tremendous, really, really good. Only I drew her ire. This is no way to have a marriage, and as miserable as it was for me, it was just as frustrating and unsatisfying for Loretta, too, I am sure. How could it not have been? For some bizarre reason we brought out the worst in each other. The strangest thing of all was that after we divorced in the mid-1980s, we got along fine. We no longer argued. Whenever we met, it was cordial and it was genuine. We caught each other up on news about the kids and the extended family and actually had a decent relationship.

I once got an insight into how we tended to be polar opposites. Someone who knew both of us said to me, "Loretta's game is to be contrary to you in any and all matters." He then said that if I remarked, "Gee, it's a nice day," Loretta would immediately jump in with, "Now, Ron, it's not that nice and you know it."

Then he instructed me in how to see this dynamic for myself. Sometime later, Loretta and I were talking and I brought up a point about something, an opinion that I don't remember now. Loretta immediately took an opposing stance. We continued talking, and about ten minutes later I brought up the subject again, this time taking the perspective that Loretta had taken the first time. She immediately countered it by taking up and asserting my original point. That sums up our nearly 30 years of marriage. Perhaps the bottom line is that we both wanted different things out of life.

The strife between us never seemed to interfere with our relationships with our kids, however. Both of us loved them equally for the individuals they were. All the kids were active, Denise and Lori with their dancing and Ronnie and Dave with sports. Despite his small size, David was strong. I used to lift him up so he could grab hold of the molding atop a doorway, and he could hang there by his fingers, even as a toddler.

When Dave was young, he was a good kid around the house. He had a great sense of humor and we pulled a lot of pranks together. One time, I got him up on the garage; he was wearing a pair of my red Speedo swim trunks with newspaper stuffed in them so they'd stay up, hiking boots, one of Loretta's wigs and a kite that looked like a Batman cape, and he was holding a toilet plunger pointed toward the sky. We took a photograph of him and gave it a caption of "Super Geek." He loved doing goofy stuff like that and went along eagerly. In addition, he was a very smart kid in school and a good talker, extroverted and willing to state his viewpoint.

At home David was subject to the discipline of his mother and me. In school, however, things were different. There he was a wiseass who had the habit of taking verbal potshots at the other kids. Eventually, the other kid would tire of the abuse and try to put a stop to it, which apparently resulted in what David wanted all along—a fight. Ordinarily, the smaller kids are the ones who are bullied. In David's case, that was not always so. Often, he came home with tales of a scrape he had been in that day. Another negative trait that he seemed to possess early on was a habit of denigrating other people. He would come home from school complaining about other kids. It became almost a regular occurrence.

He'd walk in the door and begin griping about something a kid had done or someone he had a problem with. Though I had no idea at the time, this would become his signature style when he took charge of Scientology many years later.

As a father, though, I supported all my kids unconditionally and was invariably protective of them. That is probably why I never bothered to look too deeply into that red flag waving wildly during David's childhood. It is a characteristic I became all too familiar with later on. Ronnie told me that he has been in four fistfights in his entire life, and three of them involved protecting his little brother from situations that Dave had instigated.

SIX

DAVID'S MIRACLE

GROWING UP, ALL MY KIDS EXCEPT DAVID WERE HEALTHY. His cross to bear was a bad case of asthma, and this plagued him all through his early years. The affliction became apparent when he was an infant, just months old. He couldn't exhale, and the attacks became fairly common. Asthma sufferers can get the air into their lungs but can't force it out, and it is unsettling to see someone having an attack, especially a child of your own.

His pediatrician administered shots of adrenaline to relieve his gasping. I didn't want to keep taking him in for shots because I had heard this was not too good for a kid, so I was always on the lookout for other ways to deal with it. Not to mention that he screamed like a banshee when jabbed with the needles.

Asthma made him miserable. It really ruined his life for several years. In the beginning he might have an episode every six months, but they became more frequent as he got a little older. He'd have attacks at night and would be up, unable to breathe and crying. It was heartbreaking to see because he was an otherwise happy kid.

It got so bad that one time in the middle of an attack, he started turning blue. He couldn't breathe out, and Loretta and her sister, both of whom were nurses, stood there saying, "Oh, my god!" but doing nothing. Finally, I smacked him on the ass and he cried, which forced him to exhale and that stopped the attack. Afterward they criticized me for being cruel, which really ticked me off because they were just standing there. I would have done anything to help him breathe normally again.

When he was about five years old, one attack was so bad that he wound up in the hospital in an oxygen tent. I felt helpless as I watched him lying there, his chest heaving as he struggled to breathe. He was there for a couple days, and I bought him a stuffed monkey so he would have a companion to share his isolation.

Later, in the middle of winter, another attack came on. His mouth was open, but he literally could not breathe out. Again, he began turning blue. This was serious. I had an idea. I grabbed him in my arms and ran upstairs to the bathroom. I stripped off his clothes and turned on the shower. It wasn't going to be pleasant, but I had to do something. I took off my clothes, too, grabbed David in my arms and stepped into the shower. I didn't want him to think he was being punished by what was about to happen, so I went in with him.

"Listen," I said, "I know this is going to be horrible, but I've got to do something to help you."

I was holding him in my arms as the warm water washed over us both. Suddenly, I slammed off the hot water and we were both instantly shocked by a blast of ice-cold water. David's gasp reflex kicked in and he began panting uncontrollably. So did I, believe me. It was painful for both of us, but the attack was over. I got a big Turkish towel and dried him off. I could feel his racing heart return to normal, and the goose bumps receded. My own fears ebbed as I saw that my little boy was going to be all right. I gave him a kiss, and he was okay after that.

I knew these measures were only temporary and that he would suffer another attack, so I was always looking for ways to get at the cause of it. I was only dealing with the symptoms as best I could. The doctor who gave him the adrenaline shots was only treating symptoms too. I wanted to find out what the hell was causing these attacks that were messing up his life so much.

I found out about a specialist and took David to see him. The specialist said that skin tests had to be done. We took off David's shirt and he stood between my knees facing me. The nurse took a board about a foot square that had more than 30 needles on it and pressed it against his back until each needle drew blood. I witnessed this and thought, You bastards, this had better result in something positive. Then she took a tray with a large number of bottles and, in order, daubed a bit of solution from each bottle onto each of the breaks in his skin. The doctor came in, inspected the reactions and told us to come back in a couple weeks for the test results.

Two weeks later we went back, and the doctor's diagnosis did not fill me with confidence. He said that David was allergic to the bacteria in his throat, which made no sense to me at all. From the rather fumbling way the specialist explained it, I got the distinct impression he was grasping at straws. Why were the asthma attacks intermittent and random if the bacteria were in his throat all the time? This specialist did help in one way, though: his diagnosis validated an idea I had been considering, which was that David's asthma attacks were in some way psychosomatic.

Sometimes, when I saw that an attack was coming on, I took him out to the garage and made him lift weights. Often, it would stave off the attack. The idea came to me one day as I thought back to something that had happened to me in the Marine Corps.

I had gone to the base dentist for some work on my teeth. A week later, my face began to hurt every afternoon at 4:30. It felt like my face was in an iron mask. Each afternoon this pain would murder me. I went back to the dentist and he said, "Oh, yeah, that's facial neuralgia." He gave me some aspirin and sent me away. He could name it, but he couldn't solve it.

The next day at 4:30 my face started killing me again. I knew I had to do something, so I put on my fatigues and walked out to the air station gym. I figured that instead of moping around, feeling pity for myself, I would go take a workout. There was another guy in there and I said, "You want to lift weights? We can spot each other."

We began lifting. He spotted me on a set of bench presses. Then I spotted him. Then he spotted me. Then I spotted him. Then . . . wait a minute, I thought. My face no longer hurt. The pain had gone away. I just sat there on the bench trying to figure out what the hell had just happened. I came up with a theory: pain must need your attention to exist. If you can direct your attention away from the pain, it can't continue to exist. Something threatening me like that barbell, which would crush my chest if I dropped it, forced my attention away from the pain and that caused it to go away. That was the end of the facial neuralgia. I never got it again. Amazing!

Years later something similar happened when I had a bad cold and a fever, and a buddy forced me to go skiing with him. After my third time down the mountain, my cold symptoms vanished entirely. Somehow, I theorized, if you can force your attention away from what is bothering you, it no longer has life, and this reinforced the earlier experience.

So, when David had an asthma attack coming on, if I caught it early enough, taking him out to the garage and making him lift weights often relieved the attack. Sometimes it would be 32 degrees out there in the garage. I would bundle him up, take him out there and spot him on the bench press, until he'd say, "I'm okay now, Dad. I feel better." And he would be better. Temporarily.

Around that time, in 1968, I had a friend named Nelson Sandy who sold cookware with me. One day he said, "Hey, Ron, how would you like to make an extra $100,000 a year? There's something I'm getting involved in and you should too. It's called Holiday Magic." In the 1960s, $100,000 was a fortune.

He invited me to a meeting to learn more about it. I got the pitch (it was a cosmetics marketing business) and my immediate reaction was, "This is bullshit," because all they were doing was selling distributorships, with no thought of getting products out to the consumers. Holiday Magic was one of the early pyramid schemes and went bust several years later, thanks to the Securities and Exchange Commission and Federal Trade Commission.

After the meeting, Nelson and I went to a bar for a couple drinks. He told me more about it, and the next thing I knew, I had become intensely curious. I said to myself, "You know, this just could work."

So I got involved. For a $5,000 investment, I became what was known as a master distributor. Here is the way the scheme worked: The more product you bought, the bigger the discount you got. The idea was to sell product to distributors under you and pocket the difference between your price and what you charged them. You would keep recruiting distributors under distributors and making income off the difference. There is really nothing wrong with the concept—except that everybody knows these schemes never work, though that conclusion did not dawn on me until later.

Later on, in 1969, three other distributors and I formed a so-called Holiday Magic corporate team. We were all good talkers and good at convincing others to buy into Holiday Magic. One evening, we were holding an "opportunity meeting" at the Mallard Inn to recruit other distributors. A member of our team was talking to a guy named Mike Hess, while I stood a couple steps away talking to someone else.

At one point Mike said, "Yeah, I want to get involved in this because I am a Scientologist and we believe in experiencing everything."

I overheard his remark and turned to him. "What did you just say? What is a Scientologist?"

I pinned him down and made him talk to me about it for maybe 30 minutes. The word itself interested me. I had never heard it before. He told me that Scientology was about helping people become more able in life. There were other good philosophies, he said, but the difference with Scientology was that it offered practical things you could do to help yourself.

One of the things, he told me, was that "if you become a Scientologist, you never have to take another aspirin again."

That really piqued my curiosity. "What do you mean by that?"

"Well," he continued, "if you get a headache, the way you get rid of it is look at yourself in the mirror and give the headache to the person in the mirror."

Wild idea, right? You meet some people in life, and their invariable response will be to scoff, "Nah, that's never going to work." But I have never been a close-minded individual. I have always been open to new ways of thinking or of viewing or experiencing life.

The other thing Mike told me that day was, "If you don't have a mirror handy, do this: create a mental picture of yourself looking at yourself in a mirror, and give the headache to the guy in the mirror."

Sometime later I was driving in South Jersey and realized that I did have a headache. I thought to myself, I'm going to try this. I checked around me to make sure there was no traffic nearby, and then I made a mental picture of myself looking at myself in a mirror. I gave the headache to the guy in the mirror. Lo and behold, my headache went away! Hang on a second, I said to myself. I need to check this out. This is no bullshit. This is something different. This is unlike anything I have ever experienced in my life. Therein lies the rub.

A person who is a Scientologist or who has some familiarity with the subject will understand what occurred at that moment. A person who is not a Scientologist will be absolutely convinced that I was swayed by a coincidence or talked myself into it. Regardless of anyone's interpretation, that actually did happen to me.

I had Mike's phone number, so I called and told him, "I would like to find out more about this." He sent me down to a place in Woodbury, New Jersey, Ogle's Cafeteria. A guy named Frank Ogle owned the cafeteria, and every Tuesday evening people came to his place and sat around discussing Scientology. Frank basically lectured about various aspects of life and Scientology's perspective on them.

For example, ten or twelve people would be sitting around a table, and Frank would ask the first person, "Okay, now tell me, what do you think about sex?" The person would answer, and Frank would go around the table and have each person tell him what she or he thought about sex. One person might say, "Well, sex is okay, but I only want to have sex with my husband." Another might answer, "I worry about it a little because I might pick up a disease." Someone else might say, "I'm shy in a relationship."

Then he would take something handy, like salt and pepper shakers and a coffee cup, and say, "Okay, this is you," placing the salt shaker on the table, "and this is what you think about sex," placing the pepper shaker in front of the salt shaker, "and this is sex itself," moving the coffee cup in front of the pepper shaker. "What you *think* about sex is your case"—in other words, all the person's mental reactions, attitudes, and so on about sex. Then he would say, "Sex just *is*."

That made sense to me. People's thoughts about life are not the same as looking at life directly. The next week Frank would take up another subject. After he was through talking, we would do different exercises to improve our ability to look at life and improve our communication. In Scientology these are called training routines, or TRs for short. We would sit in front of another person and just look at them until we were comfortable facing another person without feeling the need to say something. If you've ever tried this, it can take some doing. Or we might practice how to say something clearly to another person so the message really arrives. Frank might teach us how to answer a person's question or acknowledge something they had said. It was all basic stuff about how to communicate better. As I would learn later, good communication is an important fundamental of Scientology, and these exercises were my introduction to the idea.

After about four trips to Frank's Tuesday evening classes, I figured I had learned what there was to learn and I kind of drifted away. My realization was this: Everybody is trying to *create* an effect in life. Nobody wants to *be* an effect in life. So, if somebody says something to you, such as a criticism, and you give them a good acknowledgment, you can avoid becoming an effect of their criticism.

I began to use that technique to advantage in my life. Somebody would say, "Such and such," and I'd say, "Yeah, okay," and that would be the end of it. Rather than get into a long drawn-out discussion or an argument, I'd give them a good acknowledgment and shift the conversation to something I was more interested in. And it proved effective. So then I figured that if the Scientology mirror technique had gotten rid of my headache, maybe Frank could do something for David's asthma, because he was still getting attacks. Anything I had tried, including inhalers, brought him only temporary relief, and one thing I give myself credit for is that, if something is not working, I look for something else.

One day David was in class when an announcement came over the speaker above the blackboard: "David Miscavige, please come to the principal's office." He was confused—he wasn't in any trouble that he knew of. He went to the office, and I was standing there with the principal, who said, "David, you are excused from school today. Your father is taking you to see a Scientologist to handle your asthma. So, you're excused."

I drove him down to Frank Ogle's cafeteria and we walked in. I introduced nine-year-old David to Frank, told him about the asthma, and asked if he could do anything to help my son. I had heard about auditing but had never received any myself, but I was willing to try anything to get rid of David's asthma. I had to give him a chance, some hope. Maybe this will work, I thought, even though I had no idea what auditing was. Frank looked at me and confidently said, "Sure." He then took David into a back office and closed the door.

I sat down in the cafeteria and let my thoughts wander.

Forty-five minutes later, David walked out and he looked like a totally different person.

"My asthma's gone!" he declared. "It's gone!"

He was radiant. He looked confident. He was cheerful. I actually saw all those things at that moment. Something of significance had taken place in the space of 45 minutes.

That was the end of David's asthma. Throughout the rest of his childhood, he never again had a serious attack—some minor ones, yes, but never where he was gasping and couldn't breathe. It truly was an amazing occurrence, a miracle actually, considering how asthma had affected him so horribly. Nothing we had tried up to that point—the adrenaline shots, cold showers, inhalers, bench presses in the garage—had given David the confidence that something useful was being done to handle his asthma for the rest of his life—nothing until that auditing session with Frank Ogle.

Years later, I asked David what Frank did that day and he said, "Creative processing." That was an early development in Scientology, based on the theory that we create a lot of our own difficulties but that these difficulties can be overcome by encouraging the individual to re-create the difficulty mentally. Using his own creative energies, the person creates the condition, problem, situation, or whatever is being addressed. In many cases, doing so thoroughly enough will bring about a cessation or lessening of whatever is bothering the individual. I'd had a personal experience of that when I gave my headache to the person in the mirror, and my headache totally went away. That had made me wonder whether the same thing could happen with David's asthma and, sure enough, it did. Something had definitely, definitely, definitely *worked*.

The whole family could tell that it had made a big impression on David. That was *the* turning point in his young life. He decided, "This is *it!* This is valuable."

Say what you will, but there was a definite, observable change in David's health in regard to asthma. For all intents and purposes, as far as David was concerned, he was cured. And it stayed that way for years.

Imagine for a moment that you had a serious physical ailment such as David's asthma—or any number of debilitating conditions—and someone sat you down and through simple mental exercises your condition disappeared. What kind of impression would that make on you? It would literally be life changing. That is what happened to David that day, and it determined the direction his life would take.

SEVEN

GETTING IN DEEPER

MEANWHILE, LORETTA AND I WERE STILL HAVING MARITAL problems. Loretta insisted that we see our internist to find out if he might be able to help. A psychiatrist two doors down from his office did marriage counseling, so our doctor arranged an appointment for us with him. We told him our story, and he gave me tranquilizers to take. We went home and I took one. Tranquilizers are supposed to calm you down, but these had the opposite effect on me. I became intensely nervous and jittery, to a degree I had never experienced before. I flushed the rest of the tranquilizers down the toilet. "I am never going to talk to that guy again as long as I live," I swore.

Needless to say, our problems continued. Loretta said, "We've got to get help. Let's go back to the psychiatrist."

"No way," I said. "Let's go see Frank Ogle. Maybe he can help us with auditing." Basically, auditing is talk therapy as practiced since the days of Freud, though a Scientologist would object to that comparison. Still, the basic goal of both psychotherapy and Scientology auditing is to help a person resolve issues by talking about them. A therapist helps the patient stay on track to uncover the source of the problem; a Scientology practitioner guides the person being audited to a resolution of whatever the issue is.

Frank had a house out in the country, and he had grown a beard since the last time I saw him. I thought it was an effort to make himself look like Jesus.

"Frank, we need some help," I said.

"Okay, have a seat on that couch over there," he replied. We sat down on the couch. "Okay, I am going to do some processing on you. Now, Ron, in spite of what Loretta has done, can you have her?" (Meaning, I guess, could I forgive her.)

"Yes."

"Thank you. Loretta, in spite of what Ron has done, can you have him?"

"No!" Loretta did not have much forgiveness in her heart for me.

It went on like this for a while. Meanwhile, two chiropractors had come to Frank for some instruction, and they were sitting on another couch observing Frank audit Loretta and me. The chiropractors were murmuring to one another—"Oh, yeah, I see what he is doing, blah, blah, blah"—as Frank was auditing us.

At one point Frank said to us, "Just a second," and he turned to the chiropractors and said, "Listen, when I'm auditing, could you two please shut the hell up?"

We carried on for a while longer until Frank said, "Okay, this isn't working. Come over here. I'm going to put you on an E-meter."

The E-meter is an electronic device that Scientology practitioners use in auditing. The person being audited holds electrodes, and the E-meter reacts to changes in a tiny flow of electricity (around half a volt coming from the meter's battery) through a person's body. The theory is that mental energies influence the meter's tiny current, and these effects show up on the needle dial of the meter and are useful to the practitioner. (Some people who have never looked at an E-meter assert that the meter reacts to sweat on the person's hands. Of course, none of those people have ever seen some of the wild needle actions and patterns that occur during auditing, which could not possibly be caused by sweating hands. No way.) He put Loretta on the meter, meaning he turned the meter on and had her grab hold of two tin cans that served as electrodes. The meter showed that she had a high reading, that is, she was putting up a lot of resistance to the tiny current in the meter. Her reading was about 5.0. Then he put me on the meter and my reading was 1.5. In my ignorance, I immediately thought back to a chart I had seen in his cafeteria in Woodbury that showed the different levels of emotions. The level of 1.5 was pretty low on the chart, and I said to Frank, "Wait, 1.5, that's close to death, isn't it?"

"You said it, not me," was Frank's reply. He led me to believe that I was realizing I was close to death! "Some people are stuck in their head and can't get out. Some people are stuck outside of their head and can't get in. You're stuck inside your head and can't get out. That means you are in the personality of some dead person. Now, who do you think that could be?"

"I don't know. Aunt Stella? No, she's still living. My aunt Mary? No."

"Okay," Frank said, "Just try to be outside in that car," and he gestured to a car we could see through the window.

I tried but couldn't do it. "Aw, jeez, I can't do it. Man, I need a drink right now."

So Frank got a bottle of scotch and poured me a drink. Then he told me firmly, "You need auditing. I'm going to send you to somebody who's a *real* Scientologist. These people have experienced death and come back."

He gave me a name and phone number and we left. Later, Loretta called Frank and he told her, "Ron better get some auditing because he's either going to kill somebody or he's going to rob a bank," and she believed him!

Anyone familiar with Scientology knows that what took place that day at Frank's was strictly the Keystone Kops version. Regardless, that's how we got started.

The next day I went down to Norm Muller's Scientology center in Cherry Hill, New Jersey, and said, "I want some auditing." Norm Muller was from New Zealand and had been a practicing hypnotist before he became interested in Scientology. He had studied under L. Ron Hubbard in England and then moved to the United States and opened his center in Cherry Hill. I got to know Norm pretty well, and he used to tell me about his association with Hubbard, which was interesting to me. "Hubbard used to tell me to go into an auditing session and do 'A' on the person and that 'B' would happen if I did," Norm once told me, "and every time I did so, things happened just like he predicted. That gave me faith in what he had to say."

So both Loretta and I began to receive auditing. In fact, I got the whole family involved. Loretta and I would separately receive our individual auditing sessions, and the kids would do the communication drills I mentioned earlier. My wife and I seemed to have different reasons for being involved in Scientology. I was having fun, and it seemed I became more rambunctious as I received more auditing. Loretta seemed to be going along for the ride to see if it would make me a better person in her eyes. That was her main interest. In her view, I was the problem in the marriage, so it was good that I was getting the auditing. I suppose she was just going through the motions. Still, the family dynamics changed. We developed a common purpose, to learn more about Scientology. The boys were more interested than the girls, I'd say, but everyone was now involved.

My own life continued to improve as I did more Scientology. I read every book Hubbard wrote and listened to many, many of his lectures. I received Scientology auditing, and from what I learned of the philosophy in my studies and what I experienced subjectively from auditing, I gained a certainty that there was a lot of value in the subject.

In studying what LRH wrote and said, I found he was making many valid points about life, how it worked and what to do to improve things. The more I absorbed, the more I became tolerant of others around me, and to that degree my life improved. To my way of thinking, your ability to tolerate things around you has a lot to do with your ability to deal with them effectively.

The auditing also helped me a lot. I look at it this way: if something is going on in your life that may not be positive but you aren't really aware of it, you can't do anything about it because of your lack of awareness. In auditing, you begin to uncover these things, so you can do something about them. The major sour area of my life for years had been my arguments and fights with Loretta. Through the auditing, my attitude about the arguments shifted, and you could say that a lot of the wind went out of the sails. We still argued, but our arguments were never again as loud as before Scientology, and I never again even had the urge to strike her. I realized that facets of my personality made me react irrationally and were out of my control, and just that realization helped me deal with them better.

I was good at explaining Scientology to people. I used to keep a box with copies of Hubbard's book *Dianetics* in the trunk of my car and sold one to practically everybody I met. One day, I went into an Arthur Treacher's Fish and Chips restaurant and started talking to a guy. The next day, he showed up at a Scientology center in town, told the registrar that he wanted to do the Communication Course (a basic introductory course) and pulled out a check already made out for the $50 fee. The registrar later wrote a report saying that she suspected the man was an infiltrator since he already knew how much his course cost. I had told him the day before!

Years later, as I became more involved with the organization, I learned that in addition to the positive things I found in Scientology, other aspects, particularly in the way the organization was run, seemed absolutely worthless to me. Many of these I personally experienced and they were terrible. But that's getting ahead of the story. Those early weeks and months were a revelation.

By early 1971, I had finished all the courses and actions I could do at Norm's center, so I began making arrangements to travel to the Scientology headquarters, called St. Hill, in East Grinstead, south of London, for more advanced courses. Many people from the United States went to the Los Angeles center, but Norm Muller advised me, "Ron, go to St. Hill. Don't go to LA. You'll love England. They've got all kinds of quaint shops in town. You'll love it there."

So that is why I went to England. And Norm was right, I loved St. Hill. That, by the way, is where I first met the great pianist Chick Corea, who was there at the time. Chick had become interested in Scientology about a year earlier than I, and we wound up in England at the same time. One day I went into the Qualifications Division of the organization, where people went to be certified after completing a course or a level of their auditing, and Chick happened to be there.

"Man," he said to me, all bright and happy, "I just attested to Clear!"

"That's great!" I replied.

"How about a big ol' hug?" Chick said. So I gave him a hug, and that is how we met. I knew how he felt because I had just achieved the state myself and understood how great it was.

Clear is a Scientology term with a lot of baggage because it was defined as several different things at different times. Also, it was defined as an absolute state, which contradicts one of the essential principles of Scientology, that "absolutes are unobtainable." But basically Clear means that one has, through Scientology, rid oneself of hang-ups that had prohibited one from being truly oneself. One has lost the mental mechanisms that compel one to react to things unthinkingly rather than responding to them rationally. It is not that the person becomes an unfeeling automaton. Quite the contrary. A Clear is much better able to feel all of life, the good, the bad and the ugly. The Clear is less closed off to the experiences of living.

Here is how I explain it to people: You have a problem with your hand, for example. It hurts all the time. The reason it hurts all the time is because three times a day you pick up a hammer and smash your hand with it. The goal of Scientology is not to get you to a point where you can hit yourself with the hammer and it doesn't hurt anymore—the idea is to bring a person up to the awareness of "Hey, what the hell am I doing, hitting my hand with this hammer? No wonder it hurts all the time! I've been causing my own pain!" You throw the hammer away and that is the end of it. People, for the most part, make their own situations in life. Whatever condition you are in, you've thought yourself into that situation. Napoleon Hill, one of the first personal success gurus, says it in six words: "You become what you think about." Long before that, Buddha said that we are the product of our thoughts. That is a central tenet of Scientology. Your father may have told you that you are no good, but he has been dead for 20 years; you are the one keeping the recording going.

At the end of the Clearing Course, I lay down to sleep one night and . . . the mental pictures and noise that had always been there when I closed my eyes were gone. Totally gone. I jumped out of bed. Wait a minute, I thought, where is the stream of pictures I used to get? They were gone. Inside, my head was totally still. It was unbelievable. But true!

Scientologists hold up L. Ron Hubbard as the originator, or source, of everything in Scientology. He himself credited many others, including Freud, as sources of inspiration. In nineteenth-century America something called the New Thought movement sprang up. Christian Science is probably the best-known surviving offshoot of the movement. Beginning in the 1880s and persisting well into the twentieth century, many books were published by the likes of Napoleon Hill, William Walker Atkinson, Charles F. Haanel, Prentice Mulford, Wallace Wattles, Perry Joseph Green, Frank Channing Haddock, Thomas Troward and, of course, Mary Baker Eddy. These writings are full of concepts that Hubbard incorporated into Scientology. Concepts like illness begins in the mind, that we are all spiritual beings and that "you are what you think, not what you think you are" are all found in writings of the day. New Age ideas, expressed, for example, in the law of attraction and the book *The Secret,* come directly from the New Thought movement. Anyone with even a rudimentary familiarity with Scientology can pick up any book from the period and find numerous parallels.

Hubbard advances the concept of the reactive mind in Dianetics, which was the precursor to Scientology. The New Thought writers called it the subconscious mind or the subjective mind, and they described it as a mind that never sleeps and records everything that you ever experience, exactly as Hubbard explained in his book *Dianetics* many years later. Another example: Hubbard declares that the dynamic principle of existence is the urge to survive, and he divides this urge into survival for self, family, group and all humanity. Will Durant's *The Story of Civilization* describes those same dynamics. Hubbard dedicated *Dianetics* to Will Durant but gave him no specific credit for that idea.

By late April 1971, I had been at St. Hill for nearly two months and had completed everything I came to do. My time there really changed me. I was getting ready to head back to the United States. On a clear, crisp spring day I was walking outside with one of the organization's staff members. I told her, "I'm going to bring my whole family back with me next year." She thought that would be great. We parted and I began to walk away. All of a sudden snow began to fall out of a clear blue sky. It was truly bizarre. I turned back to her and she just shrugged her shoulders. Maybe that happens every once in a while in England—who knows?—but I certainly had never seen anything like it.

EIGHT

DAVID GOES TO ENGLAND

MY LIFE SEEMED UNFETTERED TO ME AS I TRAVELED BACK home. That is the best word I can think of to describe it, *unfettered*. I did not seem to have any inhibitions. I became more willing to do just about anything. It wasn't as though I turned from Casper Milquetoast into Superman, but I was less troubled by things. Emotionally, I was freer. Outwardly I may not have looked much different. Inwardly, subjectively, I felt different and it was definitely for the better, more than worth the investment I had made in time and money. By then I probably had spent about $5,000, which is a pittance compared to what dedicated Scientologists have to pay today.

My relationships with people were always good, save for my marriage to Loretta. On the way back from the airport, I had to switch from driving on the left-hand side of the road to the right-hand side, and this became a little irritating. My frustration leaked out and Loretta remarked, "I thought that when you went Clear, you would be nicer."

I let it drop. In fact, I have always been extroverted and Scientology only made me more so. I also would not back down from a confrontation if I was not in the wrong. That's how I was and Loretta knew it. Scientology had not made me more aggressive; if anything, I became less confrontational because not much bothered me anymore. I was able to let stuff roll off my back, including Loretta's barbs.

Years later she said, "I always wanted to marry a conservative guy." Wow, how much more wrong could she have gotten? Loretta mainly wanted to get married so she could have kids. Nothing at all wrong with that, and she was good with the kids, great even. She had a problem with me, something that her involvement with Scientology had no great effect on one way or the other.

I began making plans to take the whole family back to England the next year, but I had talked with Loretta about her going to St. Hill first, during the summer of 1971, just after I returned. I paid for her to take the courses I had just completed plus some even more advanced levels.

She was on board with the idea, and other Scientologists she knew were also headed over, so that June Loretta went to England to take her advanced courses. While she was away, I was working and taking care of our four kids. I thought it would be easier if I brought my mother down from Mount Carmel to help me. That was a mistake. With all due respect, looking after kids was not her strong suit.

One day, we painted the kitchen yellow with brown trim. David and the other kids helped. When we finished I asked, "Well, what do you think?"

They looked at it for a while and said, "Face it, Dad, it looks like crap."

So I went back to the paint store and bought white paint, mixed in a little blue and got powder blue for the trim and we stayed up until 2:00

the next morning repainting the whole kitchen. The first attempt had barely dried and we were at it again. The kids stayed up and helped, and this time it looked great.

The next day I got more of the powder blue trim paint, and we painted our wooden kitchen table and chairs. I had the chairs drying in the living room and my mother sat on one that was still wet. At that point I said, "Mom, this isn't working. I'm taking you back home."

Meanwhile, Loretta had not called once from England. I finally called her and asked, "How come you're not calling? How's it going? How was your auditing?"

"Oh, it was fine. It's good," she said noncommittally.

I don't think Scientology ever had the same impact on her life as it had on mine. At one point she even suggested that we move back to Mount Carmel, which would have more or less meant leaving Scientology since there was no center in the town. The most important thing in my life in those days was Scientology. Still, Loretta remained active in Scientology for the rest of her life and ascended to the most advanced levels. In the early years, though, I think her main reason for participating, as I said earlier, was her hope that it would make me a better person.

Nevertheless, after school let out for the summer of 1972, the whole family went to East Grinstead. We were there for the next 15 months, until September 1973.

We had sold the house, and off we went with all our savings. To some extent it was a roll of the dice, but I looked at it as an adventure. I was searching for a way for me and my family to make more rapid progress through Scientology. It had improved my life radically, and I felt that it would be a good way for my kids to improve their chances for success too. When we left the United States, Ronnie was 15, Dave and Denise were 12, and Lori was 10. When I brought up the idea, they were all for it. Loretta was less enthusiastic, especially because the kids would miss a year of school while in England, but she agreed that it would be good for the family overall.

East Grinstead is a pretty little town with many historic buildings, about an hour's train ride south of London. We rented a house there. The owner's wife did such a thorough job of cleaning the place for us that she even emptied the salt and pepper shakers. When we arrived, we were starving, but there was not so much as a stale crust of bread to be found. It happened to be a bank holiday, so almost everything was closed, but fortunately we found an open sandwich shop. That was our welcome to East Grinstead.

I bought a car, an Austin Westminster, that was large enough to put all four kids in the back, so we could drive the mile or so from our house to St. Hill. I always bought cars from the same guy. I made several trips to England during the 1970s and always picked up a used car from him for 100 pounds or so, real cheap. One car had a hole in the floorboard, and you could watch the road going by as you drove.

The first Scientology service we all took was a study course. Then I did more advanced auditing services, while Loretta and the kids all began training to become Scientology practitioners, or auditors. In those days the place was packed. There must have been hundreds of people studying. Today I would be surprised if there were a fraction of that; press reports indicate that the 2011 British census found only 2,418 self-identifying Scientologists across England and Wales.

Life in England was good for the whole family. On Friday nights, we usually went to a fish and chips shop for dinner. David, Denise and Ronnie became trained to audit people. Lori decided she wasn't interested, and we did not push her. She was the only child who was in school during that time. The others were doing Scientology training at St. Hill full time—that was their schooling. My view was that they would learn more of value by studying Scientology. This was a point of friction between Loretta and me because she thought the kids ought to be in school. The kids sided with me on this point, though, and we won out in the end.

Loretta, though perhaps not as engaged as the rest of us, still was actively studying on the same schedule. Her dream was to one day establish a Scientology center in the United States where the whole family could work and enjoy the togetherness she'd had with her family while she was growing up in Mount Carmel.

Meanwhile, David was enjoying his studies and doing well. He was not a troublemaker. In fact, he was a model student. He tried his best to do everything by the book. Also training at St. Hill at the time was a woman named Helen Whitney who ran a Scientology mission (a smaller version of a church that delivered introductory services) in New Jersey. One day she asked David to inspect a clay model she had made as part of a course assignment. Scientology is big on having students take a concept they have studied and model it in clay on the theory that it helps the student grasp the concept better by making it more real. For example, you could be asked to make a clay demonstration of the difference between a person and his mind. You might take some clay and mold it into a body several inches tall. You would then take a slip of paper and write *body* and stick the label on the figure. Then you might roll out a narrow ring with more clay and place this on your table so it surrounds the figure and label this new piece *mind*. Finally, you could take some smaller blobs of clay and place them inside the ring and label them *memory* to show what the mind contains. The basic idea is to make an idea more real by creating it in three dimensions. After a student makes the demonstration, another student or the course supervisor inspects it to see if it does in fact illustrate the concept.

At any rate, Helen asked David to check out her clay demonstration. David looked it over, studied it for a minute and pronounced,

"Flunk." This is what a student is supposed to say when the model does not clearly show the concept being demonstrated. Helen was taken aback and even came over to me and said, "I don't know what to say about David, but I don't know if he is in his right mind. He flunked my clay demo."

"Oh, Helen, come on," I replied. "Dave, are you going to back down on this?"

"No way I'm going back down. I don't see it in the demo."

And that was that. He was fastidious about doing everything according to standards, which is the mantra hammered into every student: "One hundred percent Standard Tech [technology]. Be standard." Standard, standard, standard. Dave bought into it wholeheartedly. A few years before, Scientology had cured his asthma, so he had a strong motivation to do things right. He took it seriously because he had personal experience with what a good application could do.

Another student was learning to use the E-meter. One of the drills consisted of calling off lists of various fruits, vegetables, dogs, types of flowers and such, and noting any reaction on the meter. The purpose was to gain practice in doing what is called an assessment, so that when it came time to do the real thing in an auditing session, the auditor could do it smoothly. Basically, an assessment is a procedure to help locate something to address in the auditing session. The auditor has a list of items that might cause the meter's needle to react. The theory is that, when the list is read aloud, the item that shows the greatest reaction is the one to address. The auditor simply calls off the first item on the list, notes whether the needle reacts and proceeds through the list until it becomes clear which item on the list should be taken up for discussion. Say a person is having problems with different people in his life. To identify the first person the auditee needs to address in the session, the auditor asks the person who he might be having trouble with, and he lists them: "Um, let's see . . . there's my father . . . my sister . . . my girlfriend, oh, yeah, my English professor . . . there's one of my roommates . . . and my mother. That's all I can think of." These might cause a reaction as he thinks of them, but if uncertain, the auditor can then simply call off each item again and note the reaction. That is an assessment and how it is used in auditing.

This student, who was not a native English speaker, had the habit of mispronouncing the word *asparagus*, which was one of the practice items on a list of vegetables. He always mispronounced it *aspa-RA-gus*. We all heard him saying this in the course room, but David was the only one who pointed it out and told him how to say the word correctly. The guy really appreciated it. David was always determined to do everything correctly, chapter and verse, and help others do it that way too.

The course ended at about 5:00 p.m. each day, and then we usually shopped for food before the stores closed, went home and made dinner. After dinner we all just kind of hung out until it was time for bed. The next morning, we got up, ate breakfast and headed off to the course again. That pretty much describes our family life for the whole time we were at St. Hill.

When I reflect on that period, I can see it was a great time to be a Scientologist in England. As I said, the place was crowded. A grassy hillside opposite the church facilities was always filled at lunchtime with people enjoying a bite and chatting, spending time with their families or just relaxing in the sun (on a sunny day, that is). We usually went to the canteen to buy something to eat and sat out on the lush grass to enjoy our break.

A fabulous camaraderie existed among the people there. We shared a feeling that Scientology was something that was going to help everyone: the world, oneself, one's family, everybody. The expectations of what Scientology could do for people were really high. It infused the entire culture around St. Hill with a positive, hopeful atmosphere. Cottage industries sprung up that manufactured leather or wooden cases to put your E-meter and study materials in. People were contributing to the movement because they wanted to, not because they were being badgered or shamed into it, as they are today.

People regularly dropped in at our house for a meal or simply to talk. Our door was always open and anybody was welcome. It was very laissez-faire living and really wonderful.

We loved going into the shops in town. The store owners definitely appreciated the extra business that Scientologists brought to East Grinstead. One time I went into WHSmith, a bookshop, to look for a particular dictionary. Hubbard placed a lot of emphasis on knowing the meanings of words you encountered in your studies, so students were always buying dictionaries. I asked the shopkeeper for the dictionary that was currently in favor around St. Hill. He said with some consternation, "Hold on, you mean you don't want the *World Book Dictionary?* Will you people please make up your minds? I've got a roomful of them in the back."

Everything about East Grinstead was different and quaint. I loved the place. Another time I went into a grocery store and asked for aluminum foil. "We don't do that," I was told. For some reason I had to go back to Smith's to buy aluminum foil! Go figure.

Housewives shopped daily for ingredients. You'd see them out pushing their perambulators, their babies' cheeks a healthy red from the chill. You could go into a store and buy a quarter of a cucumber.

Our weekends were fairly routine. We cleaned the house and went to town. The markets in East Grinstead held auctions of such things as cuts of meat, and it was fascinating to see people bidding for a leg of lamb. "I bid 15 shillings." "Sixteen shillings." "Seventeen."

Around Christmas we took a trip out to Eastbourne on the English Channel. We went to a restaurant with an enclosed porch and windows all around. We sat there and had tea and scones with double cream and jam. It was enjoyable for everyone in the family. We watched the waves churning up against the cliffs and felt the pleasure of each other's company.

When I wasn't working on my progress in Scientology, I wanted to get something going with my music. I was playing trumpet at the Dorset Arms Hotel in East Grinstead on Friday and Saturday nights. I had put together a band, and we played jazz standards, some Dixieland and popular hits, and we packed the place on both nights every week. The crowd was a mixture of townspeople and Scientologists. They loved us. The band had a positive effect on the relationship between St. Hill and the town because things were generally not good between Scientologists and the locals. For a small town (the population was maybe 20,000 at the time, at a guess), East Grinstead was home to a great diversity and large number of church denominations and other religious organizations. Mainstream Christianity had a strong presence, and it doesn't take a lot to imagine how conservative groups must have viewed Hubbard and the Scientologists' unconventional and secretive ways.

Still, I would be walking through town shopping, and random people would stop me to say, "Ron, how ya doing?"

I was known as Ron Savage. I figured that Miscavige would be too hard for people to remember. At one point the town held a contest to select a band to go to East Grinstead's sister city in France, Bourg-de-Péage. My band entered, and lo and behold, we won! Here we were, a band made up of Scientologists, and we would be representing East Grinstead in France. The *East Grinstead Courier* had this headline on its back page: "We Were Trying to Get Rid of Them, Now They're Representing Us."

We went to France for a week and had a fantastic time. People in town asked us for autographs; for that week we were celebrities. The East Grinstead Town Council was proud because the crowd loved our performances. We were invited by the Bourg-de-Péague town treasurer (which is a more powerful position than mayor because the treasurer holds the purse strings) to his home for a sumptuous meal. What a house! Marble floors and everything. We stuffed ourselves from noon until 4:00 p.m. and collapsed into easy chairs. Then he served us Pernod with water; even his kids were drinking it.

When we went back to England, the gigs at the hotel continued and so did the band's positive effect on relations between the town and Scientology. L. Ron Hubbard even went so far as to commend us for the good work we were doing, not that that was our main purpose. We just wanted to play music and earn some money.

At the time, Hubbard was living aboard a cattle steamer that had been converted into a yacht and renamed *Apollo;* he was sailing around the Mediterranean and North Africa, continuing his writing and research while conveniently staying away from government agencies that might have wanted a word with him. Most Scientologists were unaware that he was trying to avoid legal troubles. To us, he was simply the founder of Scientology and a man who was doing immense good for the world. We all held him in the highest regard, even though most Scientologists, including me, had never met him.

After we received that commendation, I wrote to him on the *Apollo* and said that we needed some help with instruments. Our piano player just played whatever piano we found at the venue. Our bass player needed a speaker for his bass. LRH wrote back and said that we were to be given whatever we needed.

By the summer of 1973, though, my money was pretty well used up, and the family had to move back to the United States. We had all made a lot of progress in Scientology, but we needed me to go back to work. There was no great sense of disappointment; that's just the way things were. Upon our return in September, we lived in Levittown, Pennsylvania, and the kids went back to school. I went back to selling cookware and still played some music. I always did well at the cookware gig. My first year selling full time, 1959, I was the fifth most productive salesperson out of 3,000 in the country. Like music, selling was something I just took to.

The kids readapted easily. They all still did well in school. Ronnie was in high school now, and David and Denise were in junior high. Denise ran for the track team and did great; she was a really fast runner. Ronnie was on the gymnastics team. David did not participate in any sports until he got to high school, and then he wrestled. His asthma was never an issue at that time. I never heard that he was bullied, even though he was still small, and he was no longer coming home and complaining about some kid at school.

There was one issue, however: a lot of kids in school were now using drugs, smoking pot, which became a problem.

One day I came home and found Ronnie sitting on a couch looking glum.

"What's up, Ronnie?" I asked.

"Nothing, Dad."

"Whaddya mean *nothing?*" I could see it all over his face that something was going on. "C'mon, what is it?"

"There is a kid at school who was selling drugs and I told him, 'If I ever catch you selling drugs to my sisters or my brother, I'm going to beat the shit out of you,' and he said, 'Well, if you beat me up, I'll have you killed.'"

I was floored. People could say and do a lot to me, but if anyone came after my family, there was no limit to what I would do to protect them.

I went upstairs and put on a pair of jeans, a t-shirt and an old jacket and grabbed a pair of leather gloves. "C'mon out to the car, Ronnie."

"Where are we going?" he asked.

"Just come out to the car. Where does the kid live?" I said as we began driving.

We found the house. "Is that it?"

"Yeah."

"Okay, come with me."

"What are you going to do, Dad?" I was steamed, and Ronnie wasn't quite sure what was about to happen.

"Just come with me," I said. We went up to the door. I rapped on it. The father opened it. "Get everybody down here," I demanded.

His wife and two kids came down. I was pretty mad. "Listen, this kid here," I said, motioning to one, "threatened to have my son killed." I demanded an apology and let them know that it had better not happen again.

The kid apologized profusely and his father said, "This will never happen again."

"Okay," I said. And we left. Ronnie never had any trouble with that kid again.

NINE

ENGLAND, AGAIN

A **FEW MONTHS LATER, IN EARLY 1974, I BEGAN GETTING** calls from the band members who were still over in England. "You need to come back over," they said. "We can do a demo and get a record deal."

Finally, they convinced me and I agreed to return. I broke the news to the family, and Loretta was dead set against it. We had a major argument about that. She wanted Ronnie to go to California to finish high school and do gymnastics, and she wanted the others to be in school. All the kids were fine about going back to England because to them it was another adventure. Fueled by the possibility of realizing the dream of getting a recording contract, I at last persuaded the family to go with me, and we were soon headed back to England. The plan was that all the kids except Ronnie would go to school this time, while he did more Scientology courses at St. Hill. Meanwhile, I would get busy trying to secure a recording contract.

One of the guys in the band said he had a contact that could get us really cheap airfares. He told me to go to New York and arrange the flights with his contact. The guy told me I could get tickets for only 50 pounds, which in those days was $125. When I met him, he told me, "You actually aren't going to get a ticket. I'll meet you at the airport and give you boarding passes, so you can just walk onto the flight." How he arranged that, I didn't know and didn't ask.

Our flight turned out to be a return charter to France. A tour had come to the United States, traveled around and was now flying home. Real nice airline. I was sitting in one row with David and Ronnie, and Loretta was a row in front with Lori and Denise. They were talking to a flight attendant, who said, "We'll be coming into France soon."

Denise then piped up, "Oh, I've never been to France before." Not something you want to say when you are supposed to be part of a tour returning to France.

Ronnie leaned over and implored, "Dad, somebody's got to stop her before she gets us sent back."

Once we arrived, we took a train from Paris to Calais and then a ferry across the Channel to Dover. We had 26 pieces of luggage, and they were stuffed with Scientology books, E-meters, paraphernalia, you name it. This was in the days when the British government was not allowing Scientologists into the country. People would be turned away at customs and have to return home. In the late 1960s British Health Minister Kenneth Robinson banned foreign Scientologists from coming to Britain to study, based on his view that Scientology's practices were "a potential menace to the personality and well-being of those so deluded as to become its followers." The ban was finally lifted in 1980, but during our times there it was not a minor concern.

I had a plan for getting us through customs, though. I went up to the immigration officer, threw down all our passports and exclaimed, "I am so glad to get away from those rude, goddamn French!" The truth is that everybody on the flight had been pleasant. Same with French customs. But I knew the stereotype and thought it might play in Dover. It did.

"I agree," the officer said. "One year," and he stamped our passports, allowing us to stay for a whole year. He could have stopped us dead. We had an East Grinstead address as our final destination.

Our next stop was customs. If they opened our suitcases, they would see Scientology books and E-meters and we'd be dead in the water. I had a plan here too.

"Okay, kids," I said, "open up every piece of luggage. He's going to check every piece of our stuff." The kids started opening up their suitcases.

"No, no, no, wait a minute," the official said. "You're okay. Go on through."

I called his bluff. He was sitting there with four aces. I didn't have even a pair. It was a gambit that I had used successfully once before.

In 1971, on my first trip to England, I was reading Hubbard's book *Scientology 8–80* on the plane. I also had my horn with me. At immigration I put down the address in East Grinstead. The immigration officer looked at the address and asked inquiringly, "You aren't one of those Scientology chaps, are you?"

I exploded, "A scientist? Whaddya mean? I'm not a goddamned scientist. I came over here to blow my horn and have a good time on vacation!"

"Okay, okay, sir," he said as he waved me through. The whole time I had the *Scientology 8–80* book in my hand, gesticulating emphatically, and he never noticed. I didn't realize I'd been holding it until I looked down. I immediately stuffed it into the pocket of my overcoat.

During this second stay, David was a good student in school and got along with others so long as they left him alone. Because he was small, he sometimes got bullied. He wouldn't take it and punched out any kid who picked on him. Around St. Hill, though, he got along with everyone. After school and on weekends, he did extra training to obtain professional certification as an auditor.

In his book *Going Clear: Scientology, Hollywood and the Prison of Belief,* Lawrence Wright claims that the family and I left David at St. Hill while we returned to the United States. This never occurred. Ronnie did return to the States before we did. Otherwise, we arrived as a family and left as a family both times we went to England.

I realize that people are not going to accept some points in my story. It is like that anytime someone writes about Scientology. If there are mistakes in here, they are unintentional. I am trying to tell the story as it actually was, and I want it to be as evenhanded and as fair as possible. I am not writing this out of vindictiveness or hate but only to shed light on my son, his character as it transformed over the years, and his behavior today as the leader of Scientology.

After someone completes training to become an auditor, they do an internship to get practical experience before the organization will certify them as fully qualified. While on his internship, David produced a higher number of well-done auditing sessions than any of the other interns for three weeks in a row and was acknowledged for that with an award: an autographed photo of Hubbard that had been laminated to a wooden plaque.

For this trip we rented a house from Quentin McDougall, a longtime Scientologist and scion of the family known for McDougalls Flour, which was as much a household name in England as Pillsbury was in the United States. He took to us and we took to him. Quentin was in his thirties when we knew him, but he, David and Ronnie got along famously. They used to play a game in the driveway with tennis balls and a garbage can lid. Quentin would stand in front of a big wall by the garage, and Ronnie and David would try to hit him with tennis balls. Quentin used the lid to fend off their shots, but occasionally they would fake a throw a couple times and then nail him good. Then either Ronnie or David held the lid and was the target, and the others threw the balls at him. Quentin had never been part of a family that was kind of rowdy, and he really enjoyed it.

We borrowed money from him to pay for the studio time to record our demos. People borrowed from Quentin all the time. He was a mark for anybody needing money. When I paid him back, he told me it was the first time anyone had actually repaid a loan.

We made three demos and I began shopping them around London. I had a suit custom made for me so I looked the part: heather green Eisenhower-style jacket, white turtleneck sweater, bellbottoms and yellow Frye boots. This was the seventies, after all.

When I went to record companies, I had a certain way of behaving. I simply assumed the characteristics of someone who already was a successful recording artist, even though all I had with me were the three demos. I would walk into an office and say to the secretary, "Hey, how are you doing? By the way, what's your A&R guy's name? [A&R stands for artist and repertoire, the record company division that hires new talent.] Oh, right, Tim. Is Tim in? Give him a buzz and tell him Ron Savage is here with some of the latest stuff I've recorded. If he wants to listen to it, I can come up now and play it for him. Otherwise, I have other people to see."

The usual response was "Okay, he'll see you right now."

"Hi, Tim. How ya doing? Ron, Ron Savage, I'm sure you remember."

That's how I got in front of people. I just acted like I was a recording artist. I smoked Havana cigars with the head of A&R at United Artists. I was on a first-name basis with the A&R people at Purple Records, Chappell Publishing, everybody. They all knew me. They assumed that

I was a guy who had been around a while and had some new stuff to play. This is something else I learned in Scientology: you assume something to be so and it will come true, if you assume it thoroughly enough. I played the role to the hilt. I always talked to the guards at the gate. I always talked to the secretaries and they would tell me their problems. I must have pulled it off pretty well because a month and a half later, we had a contract to do an album.

One day I was arriving at Polydor Records and the guard said, "Ron, Ron Savage, don't go, stay here. Listen, Gordon Gray wants to talk to you. He's going to give you a deal." (Gordon was the A&R head at Polydor.)

Then, into a phone: "Yes, sir, he's here. I'll send him right up." Then, to me: "He'll see you now. Go right up."

I walked in. Gordon said, "Wonderful stuff. We're going to give you a contract." That was it.

Three days later Chappell Publishing called and said, "We understand you got a deal with Polydor. We're also going to take you on, so we're going to give you a contract." And they gave me an advance. Two deals within days of each other.

We cut the album and Polydor listened to it. They loved it. Chappell Publishing sent a copy to the BBC. Trevor Timmer, my representative at Chappell, called me all excited. "Ron, Ron! Can you make it up here today? BBC wants to talk to you!"

You bet! I took the train to London. I was excited beyond belief. This was a dream come true. Not too many people arrive in England, cut an album and six weeks later have a recording deal and then a week after that get a call from the BBC. The significance of that in a musician's life is incalculable. Some people shop their albums all over London for 20 years and never get a deal. All this happened to me in the first two months.

Trevor and I went over to the BBC.

"Hi, I'm Bill Bebb, a producer here."

"Hi, Bill. Nice to meet you," I said, suppressing my excitement while keeping up my act.

Trevor Timmer was aghast. In the normal course of events, getting in to see a producer at the BBC was a small miracle.

Bill said, "I listened to your stuff. Absolutely great, man. Great production. I love it. I can put you on BBC for three months. I would love to do it now. The only thing is, we have to wait for two months to clear space in the schedule. But after that, how many guys do you have in the band? Ten guys? Good. You need an arranger? Okay, good. I will give you double the session fee because you're the leader, and I tell you what, I'll give you the money so you pay your guys and that will keep the Home Office off your back." (The government did not like Americans coming over and doing gigs that Brits could do, so handling it this way meant I would be hiring local people, not taking jobs away from them.)

Bill played some of the album. "Man, I love this stuff!" The album was sort of seventies-based tunes that I guess you would call easy-listening jazz but slightly out of the box. They were unique and Bill loved it.

Still in my identity as a successful recording artist, I chimed in, "Great. Glad you like it. Well, we have to go now. Don't call me. We'll call you."

Trevor nearly fainted on the spot. Bill just laughed because he was so used to people sucking up to him. He kept us there, shooting the breeze for another 45 minutes.

Things were looking really, really good. I couldn't wait to get home and tell everybody about what had happened. At the time I was doing little side gigs for £20 ($50) a pop and was running out of money. By playing on the BBC for three months, everybody in the country would know my name and I could easily make £200 ($500) for a show. The American equivalent at the time was *The Tonight Show with Johnny Carson*. If you appeared on his show, you had it made. The BBC was the same thing.

I sat the family down, and I was really excited to tell them the news. "I talked to the BBC today, and they want to put me on the air. But right now we have to wait until this quarter is up. They book shows by the quarter, and we are going to be on for three months next quarter on a regular basis. The British people are going to know me. The pubs are going to know me. This is the break we've been waiting for. If we can hang on for another two months, we will be playing on the BBC!"

Loretta was the first one to answer. "I wanna go *home*," she whined.

I turned to the kids. "What about you guys?"

"We want to go home, Dad."

Jesus Christ! I was speechless. I couldn't imagine this was happening. None of them would back me up on it. To be honest, I was devastated. I couldn't see myself sending them back to Philadelphia to fend for themselves. It was crushing for me. The BBC is not a 25-watt underground station. They were going to pay for a ten-member band, they were going to pay for an arranger, they were going to give me a leader's fee, and they were going to give me the money to pay the band.

From Loretta's perspective (and perhaps the kids' as well), going home was an opportunity to have the stable family life she desired for so long. She had done an advanced auditing training course at St. Hill and wanted me to do the same. Her dream was for the family to open a Scientology mission back in New Jersey. We would have run the center as a family and been together most of the time. It would have been ideal for her. Needless to say, when I opted to concentrate on the music, she was not pleased and it became another point of friction. At that moment, however, I was too deflated to put up much of a fight. It was five against one. I had invested so much of my time and energy to make a breakthrough, and here it was knocking at my door. Nobody else in the family could see the potential or what it meant for our future.

So, after another 15 months in England, that was it. The deal was off. We returned home to the States. Years later, David acknowledged that the whole family had really let me down.

TEN

LEAVING HOME

N AUGUST 1975, WE RENTED A HOUSE IN BROOMALL, PENNSYL-
vania, a suburb west of Philadelphia. The kids were back in school
except for Ronnie, who had moved out and was working for the Scientology mission in Chadds Ford, Pennsylvania.

Scientology's policy is that when you train to become an auditor,
you have to become ordained as a Scientology minister. David, now
15 years old and an auditor, also became an ordained minister. Once
ordained, a minister could legally perform marriages, funerals, chris-
tenings and so on. One day my sister Marcia, the only one of my three
sisters and one brother who became interested in Scientology, came to
the house and asked David if he would perform the marriage ceremony
for her and her fiancé, Carroll. Marcia and Carroll, who was African
American, had applied for a license some time before, and the license
was about to expire so they needed to get married immediately. I was
out selling and called home to check up on things. David answered and
said, "Dad, you've got to get home fast. Marcia wants me to marry her

and Carroll. When the papers find out, can you imagine the headlines? 'White Girl Marries Black Man in Scientology Ceremony Performed by a Kid'?" As I've said before, he always had a good sense of humor and was well aware of Scientology's outsider status. They eventually did get married, but I performed the ceremony since I was also a minister.

David and Denise attended Marple Newtown High School and continued to do well academically. Additionally, David was on the wrestling team and winning his matches. As far as his mother and I were aware, things were going well for him, which left us completely unprepared for the bombshell that was about to drop the following spring.

One day I came home to find him lying on his bed and looking none too chipper. Teenagers can get like that, and he was nearing his sixteenth birthday. Still, it was pretty unusual for him.

Maybe he'd had a rough day at school. Maybe a girl had turned him down. I figured I'd talk to him a bit and we'd straighten out whatever was eating at him. "What's up?" I asked.

"Dad, I can't take it anymore," he said.

"How do you mean?"

"Lookit: all the kids around me take drugs. That's the way it is. I don't want to do this anymore. I want to go help L. Ron Hubbard."

I certainly was not expecting that. What he was telling me, in essence, was that he wanted to drop out of school and move away from home, away from his parents and his brother and sisters, to join an organization that expected total allegiance and dedication to Scientology for the rest of his life and, as I would later learn, far longer. He didn't even have a driver's license, and here he was telling me he was ready to jump straight into adulthood.

I looked at him. Now he was sitting upright. His tone was emphatic. I could understand the frustrations he must have been feeling in school. High school sophomores are not the most settled bunch. Their vision of the future may not extend past their plans for the weekend. David, meanwhile, had progressed far along Scientology's strict regimen of courses and training. He was an accomplished auditor. He had jumped through the hoops and won the admiration not only of his family but of many Scientologists in England. I had always supported my children, and it was clear to me that David felt prepared to take the next step in his young life. The idea of leaving behind the burgeoning drug scene and turmoil of teenage years for something he felt would be worthwhile must have been irresistible.

"Okay, Dave," I said. "Okay. I'll help you in whatever way I can."

"Thanks. I want to join the Sea Org," he said.

"All right. I'll help you."

He told his mother and she was not in favor of it at all. She became apoplectic and rejected it outright. "I don't believe you're going to do this," she clamored. "I can't believe it!" Loretta's dream was for everyone to stay together and to open a Scientology center as a family. The last thing she expected was for one of her children to move 1,000 miles away and join the Sea Organization. She and David did not fight over it because Loretta remained in disbelief from the first moment he mentioned his plan. She and I never fought about it because it was David's doing, not mine. In fact, we hadn't fought since before I was introduced to Scientology several years earlier. While we still argued, the marriage had attained a tolerable equilibrium, so I don't think that he was desperate to get away from his mother and me. At any rate, I pledged to support him, while Loretta remained incredulous.

In those days, I was fully supportive of Scientology and the Sea Org. People who joined the Sea Org were dedicating their lives to helping humanity, I thought, looking through my rose-colored glasses. I knew that David was a good auditor and I thought he would go far. Ronnie,

Denise and Lori were proud of their brother, much like an Italian family was when a sibling joined the priesthood.

The Sea Org is comprised of the most dedicated Scientologists. They sign a symbolic contract upon joining in which they pledge themselves for a billion years of service to the Aims of Scientology, which are basically to create a world without war, crime or insanity. That is what David wanted to do. In 1967, Hubbard had left St. Hill, where he had been for nearly ten years, and had gone to sea. Ostensibly, it was to be able to continue his research, but I have read there were legal reasons as well. In 1968, Britain instituted its ban on foreign Scientologists, and this would have included Hubbard. He began buying and renovating ships to suit his needs. He invited longtime Scientologists to join what at first was called the Sea Project but by the end of 1967 had become formalized as the Sea Organization. By the mid-1970s Hubbard and the Sea Org had moved back to land in Clearwater, Florida; many of the quasi-naval traditions established in its formative years were carried on at the new land base, however. Sea Org members wore uniforms somewhat similar to those of office workers in the U.S. Navy. The organization's hierarchy more or less followed naval ranks, with Hubbard holding the rank of commodore. Musters were held regularly to account for all hands and provide general briefings. Ranks and ratings ceremonies were held yearly, and deserving members received promotions. Campaign ribbons were awarded for participation in successful projects, which were worn on more formal occasions when people were in their Class A uniforms.

I wasn't totally certain how things would turn out for David in the Sea Org, but I had always viewed Scientology as an adventure, and all my kids had done well during our two trips to England. I had gotten so much out of Scientology and had seen David helping others with it, so I thought it would be a terrific career for him. I wanted him to be happy, and I saw how happy he was in England when he was auditing.

He was bright and I thought he would be successful. I felt I had done my best to raise him to be responsible and pursue what he wanted in life. If he was ready to make the quantum leap into a new adventure, who was I to stand in his way? After all, I was not that much older when I joined the Marines, and I was fairly certain that, unlike me at Parris Island, David would not be punched in the head on his first day in the Sea Org.

I said I would help him and I did. I bought him a bunch of clothes and gave him some money. On his sixteenth birthday, April 30, 1976, David dropped out of high school, and Loretta and I drove him to the Philadelphia airport. We had his bicycle packed up in a big box along with his suitcases. Loretta still could not accept it. "I can't believe this is happening. I can't believe you are going to do it," she said over and over.

But happen it did. He got on the plane and flew to Tampa to join the Sea Org. My relationship with him did not change after that, but David himself began to change. We exchanged letters a time or two every month. In his letters he seemed to be thriving in his new life. Occasionally we would talk on the phone and he always sounded upbeat.

There is a generalization about Scientologists who join the Sea Organization that I personally observed to be true: they were people who sincerely wanted to help others and make a better world. The impulse to help is strong in most people, and I think it exists in the greater part of humanity, but there are also a relative few among humankind who would use people's kind hearts and good intentions for selfish ends. You could even say that good people are flawed because they have a hard time conceiving that others are not also basically good and therefore can be deceived.

That is the general environment that David entered when he went to Scientology's then-worldwide headquarters in Clearwater, Florida, in May 1976. Anyone who has left home and gone away to college knows what freshman year is like with parents no longer around. I am sure that David felt that same sense of liberation too.

The year before, the church had bought a decaying but well-known Clearwater landmark, the Fort Harrison Hotel, plus another local building and set up shop. Scientologists began going to Clearwater for auditing or courses, a far more convenient arrangement than going to the *Apollo,* which was always moving about the Caribbean, having crossed the Atlantic a year or so earlier. They stayed in the hotel's rooms and did their courses or auditing in repurposed cabanas or in the tenth-floor ballroom, which had been converted into a course room.

The new facility became known as the Flag Land Base. *Flag* refers to the eight years when L. Ron Hubbard lived aboard ships in the Mediterranean and Caribbean, and the *Apollo,* his home, was the flagship of the Sea Organization. The base in Clearwater became the new center of Scientology activities, even though by the next year Hubbard had moved out to California, two and a half hours east of Los Angeles near Palm Springs.

Every six months or so, I went down to Flag from Philly, and David and I always met and spent time together. Our relationship was the same as it had always been. Each time I was in town, he made a point of coming to see me, and I could tell that he was happy and doing fine. It made me proud. The only change I noticed was that he was very dedicated to his job. He would have to run off somewhere and, since Sea Org members did not make a habit of sharing all the details of their jobs, I did not know much about what he was doing. The Sea Org tended to operate on a need-to-know basis, meaning Sea Org members did not share details about ongoing projects and upcoming plans. But I knew he worked in the part of the organization called the Commodore's Messenger Organization (CMO). The unit got its name from Hubbard's rank of commodore and derived from a communications system he established while at sea. Aboard the *Apollo* were several children whose parents were members of the Sea Org and served aboard the ship. Hubbard began using these youngsters, preteens or young teenagers, to carry messages for him to various parts of the ship. In time they became an official adjunct to his office and gained status because of their closeness to Hubbard himself.

In Clearwater, the CMO retained its status as the senior administrative arm of the base. Although David was never on the *Apollo* and had not yet met or worked with Hubbard, he was a bright, energetic young man and became a natural fit with the CMO. He adapted easily to the Sea Org. His dedication to whatever task he was assigned made him popular with others, though I have been told that he was more focused on his work than on socializing with the other messengers. Still, he fit in well, and for a while he had a girlfriend who also was a messenger. He was friendly with his roommates in his dorm and shared their interests in music and sports. Often, he and his friends would skip lunch and instead go swimming in the hotel pool, then change and be ready for the afternoon roll call.

In the mid-1970s, CB radios were popular and the messengers had CB handles. David's was Puppy Breath. This is evidently because his older brother Ronnie had the CB handle Dog Breath back in Philly.

So, early in his career, David acquired status as a messenger. He also acquired a taste for power. Messengers already had a certain amount of altitude and therefore power, quite a bit actually; they even had authority over longtime Scientologists, many of whom had been in Scientology for decades and had reached its highest levels of auditor training, executive status, and auditing advancement. This was probably a big mistake on Hubbard's part, since it meant that young people without a lot of Scientology experience were making important decisions based on their position as Commodore's Messengers but not a lot of personal experience with Scientology, its technology or administrative policy. The value of status over experience was a lesson David absorbed early on, and it became encoded in his DNA. Looking back on it now, I am sure that this is when he began to change.

Someone who was there at the time related a story to me that illustrates the point. At the time, David shared a room with two other young staff members who were around his age. One evening, they were in their room on the ninth floor of the hotel during the dinner hour. It was time to head downstairs to the after-dinner roll call, which David presided over. The elevators were crowded and slow, and David worried about being late, which would not look good since he was responsible for taking the roll. So he bolted down the stairs, nine flights to the mezzanine where the muster was held. His roommate checked his watch and figured he still had time to take the elevator. And, sure enough, when he got off the elevator, he still had time to spare. David, however, had already begun taking roll and chewed out his roommate, with whom he was quite friendly, for being late, when clearly he was not.

Authority agreed with David, and his ambition was to climb as high as he could in the organization and ultimately work with L. Ron Hubbard himself.

Scientology has different bodies of knowledge. One is the technology of auditing another person. Also, the organization is run on administrative principles. Then there are bodies of knowledge that are specialties of the Sea Org, and one of these is mission technology.

A mission, in Scientology parlance, is a task that needs to be done outside routine operations. People selected to do missions are called missionaires, and they receive training on how to execute their duties on a mission. Missions can be "fired" into areas that are troublesome or not doing as well as expected, as well as to implement new systems or for any number of other reasons. Say, Hubbard had developed a new auditor training course, and it needed to be exported to organizations around the world so they could begin to use it to train students. Missions might be sent to organizations to implement it and see that it was being run smoothly. Or, if an organization was foundering and had few people coming in for courses or auditing, a mission would be fired in to find out what was wrong and put things right again.

David, just turned 16, was selected to do a mission locally at the base in Clearwater to straighten out an area that needed fixing. I am told by someone who was there at the time that David was criticized on that mission because he and the person he was working with were engaged in "stat pushing," an action that refers to statistics and has a bad reputation among Scientologists. Statistics are the numbers that reflect how something is doing administratively. Clever people, however, can learn to manipulate statistics to make themselves look good, and this is what Scientologists call stat pushing. They regard the practice as akin to a corporation that focuses solely on turning a profit for shareholders at the expense of the environment, employees, consumers, and society at large. In this instance, David and his colleague were counting jobs as completed when they actually were not. David was guilty of stat pushing, and it eventually caught up with him. A senior executive from that time told me that David's mission was terminated and labeled a "failed mission," in other words, unsuccessful. Still, I think that David liked the taste of authority. I cannot say for certain, but I suspect that a desire for more and more power was kindled right there in his early weeks and months in the Sea Org.

In 1977, David was transferred to the secret base in La Quinta, California, where LRH had moved, 20 miles southeast of Palm Springs. David became part of a small group of messengers who were there with Hubbard and a larger group of about 50 other Sea Org members who cared for the facility and maintained Hubbard's communication channels to the rest of the Scientology world. David's duties were handling the administrative traffic to and from Hubbard. Again, he fit in well and proved himself to be an energetic team player and popular with the other messengers.

Though I did not see him again for a little more than a year, we wrote letters and shared news about what was going on in our lives. In one letter he said that he had moved to a new base that was in a confidential location but that he was doing well. That was how I found out he had left Florida. I figured, That's the way it is in the Sea Org, and took it in stride, especially since it was obviously a promotion. If the location was confidential, it must mean that he was doing something out of the ordinary, and I took that to mean that he had gained a measure of trust from the organization. By this time, Loretta had resigned herself to the fact that David was doing what he wanted, and they remained in touch occasionally.

For years, Loretta and I had been considering a divorce, and I agreed to move out in 1977. I got an apartment in Upper Darby, near Philly. David got a leave from the Sea Org the next year and stayed with me for a week. (He wasn't upset that Loretta and I were separating. In fact, the kids often commented that we should have divorced long before.) I was really looking forward to seeing him again and drove to New York to pick him up at JFK. When I saw him, I approached to give him a hug but he stopped me in my tracks. "Before you hug me, I have a message for you. Today before I left, we were on the film set and I was dressed in this suit. LRH said to me, 'Hey, you look good, Misc. Where are you going?' I said, 'I'm going on leave, sir.' He said, 'Well, have a good time.' And just as I was walking out the door, he called out, 'Misc, say hello to your old man for me.'"

Now, here's how that came about. After the band and I cut the album back in England in 1975—its title was *Freewheelin' Ron Savage*—I sent a copy to LRH as soon as it came out. One Christmas at the La Quinta base, Dave was on messenger duty, helping Hubbard deal with his traffic, and the album was playing when David came into Hubbard's office. He had a wall filled with albums but mine was on the turntable. Some years later, his public relations officer told me that Hubbard really liked it. In fact, he told her, "Now there's a trumpet player. See if you can get him."

I was so exhilarated at seeing Dave and receiving the greeting from LRH that I got lost leaving the airport, and it took us more than an hour longer to get home.

That was the start of a really great week for David and me. We spent the whole week doing nothing, just going out for meals, talking about Scientology, about what Dave was doing and how he enjoyed it, talking about the Philadelphia Eagles, talking about life. It was a really enjoyable time for both of us.

The new facility where he was stationed, known as Winter Headquarters, was a former resort where burned-out business executives could recuperate. It had swimming pools, a tennis court and several buildings that served as living quarters, but its chief advantage, so far as Hubbard was concerned, was that it was very hard to locate, although it was right across the road from the posh La Quinta Country Club. Anyone looking for L. Ron Hubbard would have had a difficult time finding him among the tamarisk (salt cedar) trees, date palms, scrub brush and blistering temperatures. Since leaving St. Hill in 1967, Hubbard had maintained a low, even secretive, profile. His whereabouts were not generally known to Scientologists or, perhaps, government agencies. While his picture hung in every Scientology organization in the world, I have been told that when he moved to La Quinta, his appearance changed dramatically. His hair, still red, had grown down past his shoulders. He sported fluffy muttonchop sideburns and a Colonel Sanders goatee, and he dressed in bolo ties and cowboy hats and boots, giving every appearance of a gentleman rancher.

In an effort to blend in with the locals and remain as inconspicuous as possible, La Quinta staff members did not wear the usual naval-style uniforms that other Sea Org members wore in Clearwater, Los Angeles or other locations that delivered Scientology services. Everybody at the La Quinta base used fake names, and when they went into towns such as Palm Springs or Indio, they were strictly forbidden from using any Scientology terminology. Meanwhile, inside the facility itself, Scientology operations continued as usual: staff received auditing, meals were served, the facilities were renovated and maintained, and Hubbard continued to direct the growing worldwide Scientology network.

In 1978, when David was 18, Hubbard began an ambitious project that had been on his mind since his days in England: training films to demonstrate different aspects of the auditing procedure, such as communication protocols and how to operate the E-meter. Since only about 70 people were on the base at that time, nearly everyone had a job in the filmmaking operation as well as another administrative duty. David worked as a videographer in Cine, as it was called; administratively, he was a project operator. This meant he oversaw various projects, run either locally or in remote areas of Scientology, such as ensuring that construction of a new building was completed or implementing a new promotional campaign in churches around the world. People have told me that this was the first time they noticed a vicious streak in him, when he sent nasty communications to people working for him. He began getting cocky, as I was later told; it wasn't apparent to me at the time in his letters or any phone calls.

Each morning, the orders of the day were issued, giving the day's schedule, items of interest and usually some notice from Hubbard himself. One day Hubbard inserted a message about showing compassion for others. Another messenger saw the item and thought that it might give David some pause, so she put it in his basket in the communications center where people's mail was delivered. When David saw the notice, he became outraged and spent the next several hours tracking down who had put it in his basket and why. It obviously had struck a nerve.

Like anybody else, David was not immune to getting into trouble occasionally. One time he was involved in a car accident in town. A fender bender is no big deal, but anything that might compromise the security of the base was serious indeed, so David had to spend time working in the messengers' vegetable garden as punishment before he was allowed to resume his regular duties. Another time he lost his keys, which was considered nearly a capital offense because, again, it potentially compromised security. Anything that anyone did to breach base security was considered quite serious, though David, in his cockiness, seemed unaffected by the transgression.

It is important to know that the Sea Org has its own culture, rules and regulations, which are quite different from those in other echelons of Scientology and from those in society at large. As one climbs the Scientology hierarchy, everything becomes stricter. At the lower-level organizations, or missions (not to be confused with Sea Org missions, which are temporary assignments rather than an organizational structure), relatively little control is exercised over staff members or parishioners apart from the requirement that Scientology be correctly applied. As one moves into a full-fledged church, there are more stringent controls because the auditing and training materials are more complex. Joining Sea Org is akin to joining the clergy of Scientology and, as in a monastery, it has a whole other set of rules and regulations. Temple monks, unlike Buddhist laypeople, for example, spend several hours each day meditating. In the Sea Org, people eat communally, wear uniforms, live in dormitories if they are not married, maintain tight schedules, learn that transgressions of group mores are dealt with more severely, and so on.

One of Hubbard's original messengers aboard the *Apollo* was a young woman named Michelle Barnett. She and David became attracted to each other and were married at the end of 1980 when she was 19 and David was 20. Loretta and I did not attend the wedding, since it occurred at the confidential Sea Org base out in California, but when we finally did meet Michelle, we both liked her immediately. She was known to everyone as Shelly, and for many years she was David's closest confidante. As David attained more and more power, Shelly rose with him. Fiercely supportive of her husband, she adopted many of David's characteristics as time went on. While my interactions with her were always cordial, I have to say that our relationship was rather distant, even after many years as daughter-in-law and father-in-law. Business always came first with her, and socially she was somewhat reserved. The Internet is rife with claims about how David allegedly "disappeared" his wife some years ago, but I knew nothing about it. David never talked to me about his marriage or any problems he and Shelly had, and after 2004 or 2005, I never saw Shelly in person and never knew where she was. As I have mentioned, the Sea Org operates on a need-to-know basis, and if there was a marital rift at the very top of Scientology, you can bet that I would not be privy to it, father or not. I will say, though, that I don't doubt for a minute the stories I have read that Dave banished her to one of the church facilities in the mountains above San Bernardino.

I can add one detail, however, and it may shed some light on the story. Shelly and I have birthdays one day apart, and we regularly exchanged cards and presents through the church mail system. Shelly always acknowledged my gifts, and I normally received a thank-you note the day after. Around the time David is said to have had her banished—something I knew nothing about—I sent her cards and gifts as usual, but her replies now came a few days later. A former staff member told me recently that he used to see my presents in the mail center in the basket for the facility near Lake Arrowhead in the San Bernadino Mountains, where I believe Shelly has lived since about 2005.

I get the sense now that in the early 1980s David began to use the system for his own ends. In early 1979, L. Ron Hubbard, then 68, moved the base from La Quinta to the former Massacre Canyon Inn resort in Gilman Hot Springs, which is just outside Hemet, California. While the La Quinta facility is in the low desert near Palm Springs, which is miserably hot for six months of the year, the new base is at a higher elevation, farther west and, while still hot in summer, has a generally more temperate climate. Instead of the bare rocks and scrub brush of La Quinta, the new location had considerably more vegetation. Hubbard never lived at the new base. Instead, he took up residence in apartments in Hemet, and his whereabouts were not known to the general staff, only to the messengers, including David, and a select few others.

For the messengers, having to service Hubbard in one location while also being held responsible for carrying out their other duties at the base subjected them to a lot of stress, shortened sleep schedules and so on. David used his management duties as an excuse to free himself from working at Hubbard's remote location, and the messengers began to notice that he was separating himself from others and acting as if he were superior, or as though the normal group expectations did not apply to him.

In the fall of 1980, David had had a serious asthma attack, so bad that he was taken to the emergency room at the hospital in Hemet. While in the hospital he said that he had a major realization about power. "Power," he said, "is not granted. It is assumed." That seems like a strange epiphany to have during an asthma episode. Nevertheless, it became the tenet that took him to the top of the organization. What happened was relayed to me by people close to him at the time. That insight became his operating motto, and by 1981, David had elevated himself to a position that effectively removed him from oversight of anybody in the Commodore's Messenger Organization. To use a football expression, he saw daylight and broke for it with everything he had. Thus began what I think was an unholy alliance between him and L. Ron Hubbard.

ELEVEN

CLIMBING THE LADDER

DESPITE ANY APPEARANCES TO THE CONTRARY, SCIENTOL-
ogy as an organization was never run the way conventional groups
operate. L. Ron Hubbard did things his way, and the organization that
formed around him reflected that. For most of 1980 and 1981, Hubbard
was writing books in seclusion with only two aides to assist him, Pat
Broeker and his wife, Annie. She was a longtime messenger; her tenure
went back to the days on the *Apollo*. Hubbard's absence was referred to
as "being off the lines," meaning he was not regularly on the normal
channels of communication. Essentially, he was allowing the messengers that he had trained over the years to run Scientology internationally. He spent the next 20 months living in his Greyhound bus–sized
motor home, assisted by the Broekers and writing his last novels.

During this period, Pat Broeker occasionally met with the head of
the messengers, a young woman named Dede Voegeding. The meetings
usually took place at night at predetermined locations, most often in the
Los Angeles area. To ensure Dede's safety, David or another man would

drive her to the meeting location. Pat and David were old friends from David's early days at the La Quinta base, and they renewed the friendship during these encounters. Shortly after David began accompanying Dede to these meetings, Hubbard removed her from her post as head of the CMO. Although she could not say for sure, Dede told author Janet Reitman, when interviewed for Janet's book, that she believed Hubbard had been fed false information about her. Dede was replaced as the head of the CMO by her sister, Gale Irwin.

Concurrent with Dede's removal, David moved into a post called special project operator, or Special Pjt Ops, which was mainly concerned with defending Hubbard against the litany of legal actions being filed against him by various agencies. The most notable stemmed from the FBI raid of the Los Angeles church headquarters in 1977 that revealed massive infiltration of the government by Scientology operatives. Upon assuming the duties of Special Pjt Ops, David began reporting to Hubbard himself through Pat Broeker. David was now autonomous from the CMO, answering only to Hubbard. I think back to that day when David told me he wanted to go help L. Ron Hubbard, and clearly my son was realizing his ambition. After this promotion, I have been told, his attitude became brasher and less respectful of those with whom he worked. His firecracker personality had fewer and fewer checks and balances. A mean streak appeared, as did a bossy attitude. I can speculate that the more power he got, the more he wanted.

His assumption of the Special Pjt Ops position opened the door for David to get rid of another potential rival, Hubbard's wife, Mary Sue. She took the fall for Hubbard after the 1977 FBI raid and eventually ended up going to jail to protect him, as did ten others, all convicted of conspiring to steal documents from the U.S. government. Hubbard had said that Mary Sue should leave her post as head of the church's Guardian's Office (its legal and public relations arm) to concentrate on her legal case. Before Dede was removed from her job, she and David had argued about how Mary Sue's stepping down should be handled. David wanted her made an example of in an effort to further distance Hubbard from the fallout of the raid, while Dede wanted to protect Mary Sue as much as possible and let her slip quietly away from the limelight. With Dede's removal, David's means of dealing with Mary Sue won out, and he had her ostracized and later purged from many Scientology records, no easy task since she had been Hubbard's staunchest confidante as well as his wife from the early days of Dianetics and Scientology. No one had supported Hubbard through the years more than Mary Sue.

Hubbard often prefaced his lectures with casual remarks about goings-on around the organization at St. Hill or in Scientology in general, and he often mentioned Mary Sue's name. These mentions have since been edited out of Hubbard's lectures. Every church in the world maintains a public showpiece referred to as an "L. Ron Hubbard office." These are there to maintain Hubbard's presence symbolically as the "source" of Scientology. On his desk were always photographs of his wife and children. These have been removed as part of purging Mary Sue from the records. When she died in 2002, any mention of her passing became conspicuous by its absence. The usual practice when a Sea Org member dies is for the Executive Director International to issue an "In Memoriam," which informs Scientologists of the death, detailing the deceased's contributions and thanking them for their good work. The order to ignore that protocol in Mary Sue's case could have come only from David. How much her being banished from the Scientology she did so much to help create contributed to her relatively early demise at age 71, I cannot say, but I personally think it could have been a factor.

In late 1981, Hubbard resumed regular communications with the organization, and he asked for reports to be sent to him summarizing every aspect of Scientology operations, from legal situations to how organizations around the world were faring to matters at the local facility in Gilman Hot Springs.

As the head of the CMO, Gale Irwin had overall responsibility and authority for sending the reports to Hubbard. She also had the entire Scientology network to command, so when there were meetings with Pat Broeker in which she had to deliver reports and other administrative items for Hubbard and receive his responses to earlier reports, on a few occasions she let David meet with Pat alone. These meetings were often time-consuming affairs. For security purposes, Gale first had to go to a public phone booth at a prearranged location somewhere in the Riverside–San Bernardino area. Pat Broeker would then call and tell Gale where to meet him so he could get the reports and pass along to her Hubbard's responses to the earlier reports. Usually they met in Los Angeles, often near LAX. With this complicated protocol, the hours of driving and the meeting itself, a single meeting with Pat chewed up most of the workday, and Gale found it difficult to spare the time to do it.

In time, Gale became concerned with David's unbridled ambition and unruly behavior. She alerted the most senior technical person in Scientology, David Mayo, to interview David to find out what he was withholding from his colleagues and to "clean him up," Scientology jargon that means to get him straight with the group again. David refused to submit to any sort of dealings with Mayo and stormed into Gale's office. She confronted him about his behavior, at which point (she later told Janet Reitman) David became furious and physically tackled her, sending her through an open door. At this, Gale became alarmed and arranged to meet with Broeker to have David removed from his post lest he jeopardize the tricky legal position Hubbard was in, not to mention the disruptions David was causing locally with his behavior.

According to several accounts, Gale arranged to be driven to a phone booth to await a phone call from Pat about a meeting. When David found out where she had gone, he packed several of his associates into a van and raced to head Gale off. When the van arrived, one of the group used a tire iron to destroy the pay phone, making any contact with Pat impossible. As Gale recounted it, David then nagged her to get into the van. There he trashed her verbally while the others mostly looked on in cowardly silence. Gale was removed as the head of the CMO and replaced by a more malleable messenger named John Nelson, someone who had worked with David when he headed up the area responsible for running Sea Org missions. Any perceived rivals were now out of the way.

One final story from around that time illustrates that life within David's widening sphere of influence was becoming increasingly serious. Around Christmas time the messengers got into the spirit of the season by drawing names from a hat and then becoming a "secret Santa" for the person whose name they had drawn. The idea was to send little joke gifts in the days before Christmas and then follow that up with a nicer present on Christmas.

This is where a young woman named Tonja Burden comes in; she had been Dave's girlfriend for a time back in Clearwater. Tonja, in the meantime, had tired of the Sea Org and left; she was now involved in a lawsuit against the church. One of the senior messengers had a picture from Clearwater days showing Dave with his arm around Tonja. She convinced David's "secret Santa" to send this to him along with one of his joke gifts. David opened the gift and was not amused. From what I was told, he exploded and ordered a full-scale investigation to determine who had sent him the photo. That pretty much put the kibosh on the Christmas cheer for the messengers that year.

That was only the beginning. In later years and increasingly during my time in the Sea Org, Christmas became almost an afterthought. Some years the occasion was marked by the galley's preparing a nice meal and that was basically it. While there was a tree and meager gifts were exchanged, any free time to enjoy the holidays with friends and family was next to zero. The prevailing mood was intense pressure to complete the work needed to prepare for an international briefing delivered to Scientologists around the world summarizing the year's accomplishments. A friend from the base once told me that he was forced to stay up all Christmas Eve one year, as well as all Christmas Day, working on speeches for the upcoming event.

It wasn't always that grim. In the early years of the Sea Org, Hubbard presided over parties aboard the *Apollo,* and when the Sea Org moved to land, these traditions continued, especially during the holidays. People had time to shop for presents and spend time with their families. There were parties and outings. People had some time to relax. But as the years passed, people had less chance to enjoy traditional holidays, until finally they passed almost unnoticed by Sea Org members, except silently; they definitely missed having a few bright moments in their otherwise dreary lives.

TWELVE

THE WORST MONTH
OF MY LIFE

IN 1985, SCIENTOLOGY BECAME EMBROILED IN A LEGAL CASE in Portland, Oregon. A woman who had taken Scientology courses sued, claiming she had been harmed by Scientology. A jury awarded her damages totaling $39 million. It became a huge rallying cry for Scientologists around the world, and the church sent out a call to arms. They responded in what was to date the church's most high-profile event in its history. Thousands of Scientologists flocked to Portland from all over the world to protest the verdict, which eventually was overturned.

By now, David was 25 and the single most powerful figure in the church next to Hubbard, who remained in seclusion though still the head of Scientology. David and I were still in touch regularly, and he told me about what was going on in Portland. He spent weeks there directing the protest operations and the legal strategy that eventually saw the judgment overturned.

Back in Philadelphia, I had other matters on my mind. By pure coincidence, the very morning that the call to arms went out, my phone rang.

"Mr. Ronald Miscavige? This is Sergeant Rafferty from the police department in King of Prussia. We would like you to come down to the station because there's something that happened that you might be able to assist us with."

I was mystified. "Well, can you tell me what it's about?"

"Not really, but if you come down here, we can go over it."

I agreed and hung up. I turned to Loretta and said, "Listen, they want me to go down to the station in King of Prussia to go over something, but I have no idea what they want."

We drove to the station and walked in. I noticed that when we entered, the officers were looking at me but suddenly averted their eyes. Immediately my antennae went up. Uh-oh. Something's going on here, I thought.

A couple detectives took us into a conference room and sat us down. "Listen," one of them began, "there is a girl that somebody attempted to rape, and we want to know if you know anything about this."

I was floored. "Are you joking?"

"No, sir, we are serious," replied the other.

"Why would I know something about someone who somebody attempted to rape?"

"Okay, let's level with you: there was an attempted rape, and you are a suspect."

"Are you kidding me?! I'm suspected of attempting to rape somebody?!"

"Well, not only that but you are the only suspect, and we know you did it."

"Say that again."

"Yep. We know that you did it."

"You're out of your fucking minds! You're completely insane! This must be some kind of prank. What are you talking about?" I was completely flabbergasted. I could not believe what I was hearing. My fight-or-flight response kicked in big time, and I could feel the blood draining from my face, yet I had nowhere to run and no one to fight. My mind began spinning.

They showed me a composite drawing of the suspect. It could only have been me. It looked so much like me that I could have posed for the picture. I was shaken to my core. "When did this take place?"

"Last October."

"Who was the girl?"

"We aren't at liberty to tell you that right now."

Loretta then piped up, "Maybe it was Joanne . . ."

Loretta and I had been separated for a year, and I dated a woman named Joanne for a short time. Now, my own wife, with whom I had since gotten back together, was trying to help the police pin this rape charge on me! At that moment, I felt as though I had been thrown under the bus emotionally as well as physically.

The detectives got some more information from me and then allowed us to leave.

We got back in the car and I let Loretta have it. I really blew my top.

"Jesus Christ almighty! What the hell were you thinking about? How could you possibly think this of me?"

"Well," she said dismissively, "these days I'm willing to believe anything."

I was stunned. I had no idea what had just happened. After we got home, I called Dave out in Portland and said, "I don't know if this is connected with the church, but when you sent out the call for people to come to Portland, I get called by the police and accused of attempting to rape somebody."

"Listen," he replied, "you're not on your own. I'm going to send somebody with bail money. If they think they are going to fight you alone, they're up against the whole Church of Scientology."

Since David had joined the Sea Org, some of the worst in him had begun to come out, if accounts from others are credible, but that was never evident to me personally. He was supportive of me in this crisis, and we spoke often in the coming weeks. The very next day, church attorney Michael Hertzberg showed up and said he had a suitcase full of cash so I wouldn't have to be in jail as the case unfolded. The police, however, did arrest me, took my fingerprints and booked me, but I was released on my own recognizance because I had no criminal record.

Dave sent two people from the church's Office of Special Affairs (OSA), the legal arm formerly known as the Guardian's Office, to investigate the detectives on the case. It was odd that on the day thousands of Scientologists were in Portland to protest a huge damage award against the church, the father of a leader of the church was accused of being a rapist. Anyone who wanted to cast the church in a bad light could have made hay with that one. The two OSA people never could find a direct link, but there was suspicion that one detective was connected to the CIA.

People unfamiliar with the church may not know that Scientology has a branch created specifically to deal with its legal and public relations issues. This is OSA. The lawyers retained by the church to deal with its legal cases work with OSA staffers. Church representatives who address the church's public relations matters are also under OSA. This branch has an investigative unit that hires private investigators (through attorneys, to create levels of deniability) to surveil people critical of the church or of David. It has a network of church members or former staff members who spy on former members who are considered enemies, and members of this network also infiltrate and disrupt the activities of any groups that might be considered competition for the church. Now, I ask you, what other church has a spy ring? Of course, the church categorically denies this.

OSA recommended an attorney and I went to meet him in his office. The guy was laid back and mellow, too much so for what I was facing. I did not like the impression he made. I called Dave and said, "We have to get another attorney. I will go to jail for something I did not commit. This guy is no good."

The church found another attorney named Rosetti. I went to see him and he told me, "Here are my qualifications: Do you remember the Main Line rapist? He was a guy who would accost chicks and force them to blow him at gunpoint. He was caught by the state police in the act of forcing a girl to blow him with a gun to her head. I got him off."

"Main Line rapist?! Listen," I protested, "I didn't do it!"

"I don't care if you did it. I'm not a priest. I'm an attorney." At that point, I knew we had the right guy.

Shortly thereafter Michael Hertzberg visited me again. He explained how the justice system works.

"These guys need to produce statistics," he began. "If they can pin something on somebody, that is proof that they have done their job."

"But I didn't do it!" I protested.

"I know you didn't do it, but they don't care. All they want is to gather enough evidence. They need to find somebody who matches this description, and you happened to be pointed out by somebody and they are going ahead with their case."

I didn't have time to become outraged or even struck dumb by what he was telling me because at that moment two police vans pulled up in front of the house with their lights flashing. They blocked traffic on the street, clambered out and marched up to the door. Michael got up and answered the door. The officers announced they were there to search my home.

"Do you have a warrant?" he asked.

"Yes, we do." So Michael let them inside.

They began going through each room in the house. In our closet upstairs they found a box of those latex gloves that doctors and nurses use at the hospital. I had asked Loretta to bring a box home so I could keep my hands clean when I changed the oil in the car.

The cops found the gloves and looked at me knowingly. In their minds a box of latex gloves equated with my being a criminal. It was right out of a Monty Python skit, but it was not a laughing matter. My thought was, How could you be so stupid to think that because you found some rubber gloves that means I attempted to rape a girl?

For at least half an hour I followed them from room to room, answering their idiotic questions. They found a tan topcoat that belonged to Loretta. If I put it on, the sleeves would have come halfway up my forearms. They took it as evidence anyway.

From that day onward, none of the neighbors would talk to me. They had no idea why the cops came or what it was all about, yet they assumed the worst. Two vans with sirens and flashing lights will do that to people.

It was terrible. I was a complete wreck. In 30 days I lost 30 pounds. I couldn't eat. I couldn't sleep. They sent an auditor from Flag to audit me and help me deal with the stress.

Finally, it came time for the preliminary hearing. I was in the courtroom when my accuser entered. When she went up on the stand, I could see she was at least as tall as I am, if not taller. That was a small relief. Police had told me that my accuser said the assailant was at least four inches taller than she. And the woman was certainly not Joanne, as Loretta had so helpfully suggested during the initial interrogation. The case began to crumble in the courtroom that morning, and finally the prosecutor pointed at me and asked my accuser point-blank, "Is that the guy?"

She stared at me for a full minute, which was easily the longest minute of my life.

"I'm not sure."

"Dismissed!" boomed the judge. "You don't have a positive identification."

Like that, the ordeal was over. My initial reaction was relief. And then rage at the two detectives who had put me through hell on the basis of this flimsy evidence. I started to go after them—my hastily conceived plan was to punch both of them in the head. These guys should have known that they did not have enough evidence to convict me. They knew that the alleged victim could say only that she was "pretty sure" that I was her attacker. Their case was meritless. They knew that the victim had described her assailant as being about 5'10", but I was nowhere near that tall. Only a friend in the courtroom prevented me from tearing the detectives' heads off. It's a good thing, because then I really would have been guilty of assaulting someone.

Afterward, I was able to piece together what had happened. One day in late March I had gone to an apartment complex in King of Prussia. I was still selling cookware and went to the rental office to get directions to the apartments rented by the people I wanted to see. I spoke to the women in the office to get the information I needed and went on my way.

The previous October, on a night when I was home watching the seventh game of the 1984 World Series between Detroit and San Diego, someone attempted to rape a woman at another apartment complex adjacent to the first. The assailant threw her down, grabbed at her breasts and tried to rape her. Five months later, the women in the office where I had paid my visit were shown a composite sketch and they identified me as the perpetrator. The woman who was attacked was not in the office at the apartment complex in March when I stopped by and only halfheart-edly identified me in a photo lineup. I had never seen her before in my life; I was home watching baseball the night the attack occurred.

So ended the longest month and most harrowing experience of my life.

It was also the end of my marriage to Loretta. Her remark during our initial visit to the police station could not have been more of a be-trayal, and at that point I knew our marriage was over.

For some time, I had been considering joining the Sea Organiza-tion. All right, I decided, they helped me during this episode. I owe them my allegiance for that. If I join and don't like it, I will simply leave. David had been asking me for some time to join. So had others in the organization, specifically Marc Yager and Guillaume Lesevre, two of the top executives in the church. I knew I was a capable person and could contribute to the group, and, as I say, I appreciated the help the church gave me during the most stressful time of my life.

There may be other accounts on the Internet about this mess, but the account here is what is in the public record, and it is the accurate de-scription of what happened and what led up to the most interesting—and even worse—chapter of my life.

THIRTEEN

LIFE IN THE SEA ORG

BECOMING PART OF THE SEA ORG WAS NEVER SOMETHING I was overjoyed about doing. I knew it could be a rough ride. I had been around Sea Org members at St. Hill and in Clearwater since the early 1970s. I knew that sometimes Sea Org members were not paid their weekly allowance. I knew that the discipline was strict and that a Sea Org member's life was controlled to a great extent. I had been self-employed for my entire working life. I sold insurance for a time. Then I had my cookware sales. As a musician, I would receive calls to play gigs, which I could accept or not. In other words, my schedule had always been my own. I was a free spirit and an entrepreneur. This, I knew, would change when I joined the Sea Organization.

At the same time, they really helped me in my time of need. I guess you could say that I felt obligated. So, out of a sense of duty more than anything, I packed my things and drove to Los Angeles in the early summer of 1985. I knew I could offer my service and help other people and contribute to a group that had the purpose of making a better world.

The church headquarters in Los Angeles is located near the corner of Vermont Avenue and Sunset Boulevard. Purchased by the church in 1977, it was the former site of the Cedars of Lebanon Hospital. The primary Scientology organizations in Los Angeles are still located in the complex, and the former main building of the hospital serves primarily as living quarters for Sea Org staffers who work at the complex.

David got me a decent room in the building, and I stayed there while I did my orientation and introductory training. Other new recruits lived in dorms that often were overcrowded. I don't deny that being the father of the leader of the church had its advantages, at least in the beginning (and make no mistake, even though Hubbard was still alive, he was in seclusion and David was the one directing the church). During that period, Dave was spending a lot of time in Los Angeles. After the protest in Portland, another legal case was heating up in Los Angeles, and David wanted protests there as well to draw attention to the injustice, as he saw it. Because we were both living at the church complex then, we used to meet after work and shoot the breeze. Things between us were still great.

Several weeks after joining, I was brought up to the Hemet base as a new staff member for Golden Era Productions. Gold, as it is known, produces all the training films, lectures, and marketing materials for Scientology organizations around the world, and it provides support services for the management entities that operate from there. Top church management is also located on the base, so the entire compound is referred to as Gold or "Int," meaning international headquarters, or just "the base." It is all the same facility.

As I have mentioned, the facility formerly was the popular Massacre Canyon Inn resort in Gilman Hot Springs. Hollywood glitterati took mineral baths in the spa, played golf on its course and partied in the 1950s and 1960s. Then an earthquake shut off the springs feeding the spa, and people found other places to vacation. By 1978, the place was all but shut down and Hubbard authorized its purchase. The idea was to use it as a base during the summer when the desert heat in La Quinta made that place basically uninhabitable and then return to La Quinta during cooler weather. That plan never materialized, and by spring 1979 just about all of the hundred or so staff from La Quinta had moved to the new facility.

The property was large, more than 500 acres, resting right up against the San Jacinto Mountains a few miles north of Hemet. At the time of purchase, the facility had been defunct for some time. Buildings consisted of the old spa, the Massacre Canyon Inn restaurant, a tavern, the U.S. Post Office for Gilman Hot Springs, a variety of bungalows and rooms for guests, as well as various maintenance buildings. Work crews got busy renovating the rundown facilities and repurposing spaces for church management offices and multimedia productions. Since the 1960s, Hubbard had wanted to produce training films for students learning to become auditors. Western culture had grown more visually oriented, he reasoned, and he saw that being able to demonstrate various aspects of how to use the E-meter or proper communication protocols would be useful to students. Hence, his desire to script and shoot these films.

Over the years, new construction has carried on more or less continuously, and nine holes of the golf course have been resurrected. Today the place is a well-kept, sparkling facility among the otherwise drab dairy farms and horse ranches that make up most of the Hemet Valley. The central compound consists of about 50 buildings and includes a large film studio, a film-processing plant, film and video editing bays, several audio recording studios, a lavish music studio, administrative offices for Scientology's international management as well as maintenance facilities. In addition it has other sports facilities and quarters that house everybody who works there. Everything is top of the line and matches in architectural design. Hubbard said the setting reminded him of the Scottish highlands, so all the buildings follow a Scottish motif, with white buildings trimmed in blue and with blue slate roofs. Hubbard was interested and involved from afar in the property renovations (he never lived at the new base), and after his death in 1986 David ensured that building continued.

To safeguard the millions of dollars' worth of equipment as well as the staff who live there, a fence with motion sensors, cameras and spotlights surrounds the central compound. The fence is topped with razor wire, ostensibly to keep intruders out; however, the spikes point *inward,* which rather indicates that the fence is meant to keep the staff in, with the sensors and cameras to alert the security guards to anyone trying to escape.

Several times the church has attempted, to no avail, to close State Route 79, which bisects the property. Cameras continually record passing traffic to provide evidence in case of people harassing the base.

When I arrived in early summer 1985, the beginning phase of renovations was more or less completed, and the number of staff had grown from a couple hundred to two or three times that. The old Massacre Canyon Inn (MCI) became the base dining facility. Eventually, the place could no longer hold the entire staff, so mealtimes were broken into shifts, with managers seated for one shift and the Golden Era Productions staff eating at another time.

Because I was a musician, I was posted to Gold's music department as a horn player and arranger. Music was considered an important aspect of Gold. It was part of every training film or video production. Everything we produced on the base went out to the rest of the Scientology world, so it was important that it be right. And, of course, the standards were high. The Golden Era Musicians, as we were called, consisted of drums, congas and percussion, bass, guitar, keyboards, a horn section with clarinet, saxophone, trombone, and me on trumpet or cornet, as well as a vocalist.

Much of the music we produced began as ideas from L. Ron Hubbard, who years before had created melodies for various training films. We took those single-note melodies and put chords to them. After that we did arrangements and submitted these to David for approval. Upon approval we would use the piece as the title song for a film and then write other pieces that integrated with that title piece. Film music cannot draw attention to itself but has to support the film and forward its message. We were walking a fine line, but when it worked it was plain to see. Today, when I watch a movie or television show, I can easily spot when a piece of music is working or not.

One of my first assignments at Gold was making an album with Edgar Winter based on Hubbard's *Mission Earth* series of novels. I had never met a musician as competent as Edgar. He is an excellent writer, a superb musician and a fine singer. He can do it all. His knowledge of music theory and harmony is outstanding; he is one of the most creative people I have ever met. That project turned out well.

Edgar told me about playing gigs with his brother, Johnny, another fabulous musician. One time, they had a gig at some club way out in the Texas boonies. They drove for hours to get to the place. When they arrived all they found was the charred outline of the club. It had burned down the previous day, literally to the ground.

Later that year, I came out of the music studio at Gold one day and spotted Dave some distance away with an entourage of three or four people. I called out, "Hey, Dave!" to get his attention.

He turned around and didn't say a word, but he shot me a glare that said, "Who the hell do you think you are, yelling after me like that? Do you know who I am?"

Right then was the first indication that my son had changed dramatically. Our relationship was not father-son anymore. He was no longer my son but the head of the Church of Scientology and that look let me know it. The church and its operations took precedence now and would from then on out. That look of his made a considerable impression on me. My role in the Sea Organization would have nothing to do with being his father. I thought to myself, Well, I better not do that again. It was not the last time something like that would happen.

His attitude worsened over the years, but that incident was the first time I encountered it. I remember one time in particular when the Golden Era Musicians were at St. Hill for a big event in the early 2000s. I was standing backstage with Dave. Nearby was a well-known Italian pop star who was not a Scientologist but had agreed to do the concert because he supported the church's humanitarian programs.

The Gold musicians performed their show and then played dance music for the rest of the evening. I had walked off stage for a break and not 15 feet away from me and Dave was the pop star, standing with a woman who worked for the church and acted as his handler, along with two other people. David began to dress me down in a tirade that lasted nearly a full hour; the man and his contingent could hear everything as David yelled, cursed me out, and generally ripped me apart. I was totally and utterly mortified by the entire experience—the head of the Church of Scientology ripping his own father apart within earshot of others. I went numb when he began, but what I can recall was that he was upset at how incompetent we all were, how we couldn't do anything right and *blah, blah, blah, blah, blah, blah, blah, blah,* punctuated frequently with *mother—r, c—sucker* and all the rest. Meanwhile, the others stood stiff as boards, never turning around, and pretended that it wasn't happening. Had they not been able to hear David's rant, they would have been chatting with each other—it was a party, after all. They never said a word but just stood there, frozen in place by what was happening, and heard every expletive. Imagine how that might play in Italy, where family is all-important. It sure wasn't any longer to David. What must they have thought? Is this for real? Is this the head of Scientology and is that his father? The poor pop star wasn't even a Scientologist. He had come purely as a favor. The church had paid his airfare but that was it. And he had to stand for nearly an hour while David gave me an earful. The entire episode was shattering. The word *terrible* can't begin to describe how it felt.

I don't even remember the excuse he used to come down on me, but it went on until I finally said, "Okay, I got it." At that point he said, "Good. I was waiting to hear that from you. That is why I was going on for the last 55 minutes," and he turned and walked away. David and the church have always denied that he engages in demeaning or abusive conduct of this nature, but my experience plainly suggests otherwise.

Afterward, his secretary Laurisse called me into a room to do damage control. "Now, look, Dave didn't mean everything he was saying out there," she told me, trying to smooth things over. That was a standard function of hers, to come behind David after he lost control to try to patch things up. It did not matter what the reason was for his blowup. The reasons came after the explosion, to rationalize why he lost control in the first place. The actual reason, I concluded after many more similar episodes, was that he enjoyed nullifying people and that included even his father.

Over time, I found the silver lining in these thunderclouds: if you were able to simply face the music and not react, not react internally but simply acknowledge the tirade, nothing would stick to you, and when it was over, it was over for you too.

Apart from the occasional lightning strike, however, my early experiences at Gold were for the most part enjoyable. I really enjoyed working with Edgar on his *Mission Earth* album.

Then, in January 1986, L. Ron Hubbard died. The whole base went down to the Palladium in Los Angeles, where we were given the "shore story"—in other words, a lie—that Hubbard had "gone exterior"—in other words, out of his body—to continue his research without the physical body's encumbrances. Several people spoke at the event, including David, Pat Broeker and Earle Cooley, a Boston lawyer who represented the church for years.

David spoke first and announced Hubbard's passing, framing it by saying that Hubbard had done as much research as he could do in that body, had fully mapped the route to complete spiritual attainment for all Scientologists, and was now exterior and would be continuing his research free from physical limitations. While some in the crowd may have been shocked or saddened at the news, at the end of David's presentation wild applause greeted several photos of Hubbard that were shown on the auditorium screen. More applause followed Pat Broeker's relaying of Hubbard's admonishment that there was to be no sorrow, no mourning, because Scientologists know they are spirits, not bodies. The audience thus prepared, Norman Starkey, another church executive, performed the Scientology funeral service. No one addressed the issue of whether anyone would succeed Hubbard; this was a drama that would play out over the next year or so.

I attended the event and was assigned the task of acting as a bodyguard for Hubbard's son Arthur. I drove him down to Los Angeles from the base and home afterward. On the way home, we stopped at a market and Arthur bought something to eat. We got back to the base and Arthur set his bag down outside the car while we chatted for a bit. We wandered a ways from the car and the bag. That turned out to be a

David and Denise on their second birthdays
at our house in Willingboro, New Jersey.
Photo: Ron Miscavige

*David and Denise at their grandparents'
house on their fourth Christmas.
Photo: Ron Miscavige*

We often spent our vacations at the Jersey Shore. Here is a mid-60s photo with Ronnie (in back) along with Denise and David; he was a real happy kid in those days.
Photo: Ron Miscavige

Another vacation shot a year or two later: brothers by a pool.
Photo: Ron Miscavige

David, Denise, Ronnie and Lori in 1975. Five months later David was off to Florida to join the Sea Organization.
Photo: Ron Miscavige

Ronnie and David with my brother-in-law Smitty, in the late 60s.
Photo: Ron Miscavige

Dave with Shelly before Super Bowl XV in New Orleans. I can tell from his smile
that the photo was taken before the game because the favored Eagles were trounced
by the Oakland Raiders 27–10.
Photo: Ron Miscavige

The Hole. Some unfortunates spent years there in virtual incarceration, only being allowed out once a day for a shower.
Photo: Sinar Parman

A good shot of the central compound of the Gold Base looking east with numbers indicating buildings mentioned in the story: (1) Music rehearsal studio where I worked for 26 ½ years of my life. (2) The Hole, two sets of double-wide trailers that held Scientology's top international managers before David dissolved them in 2004 and restricted everyone to the building. (3) Massacre Canyon Inn, which is the dining hall for the base. (4) The old health spa, which has served as the enhancement building for the base since the property was purchased in 1978. (5) The berthing buildings, where Becky and I

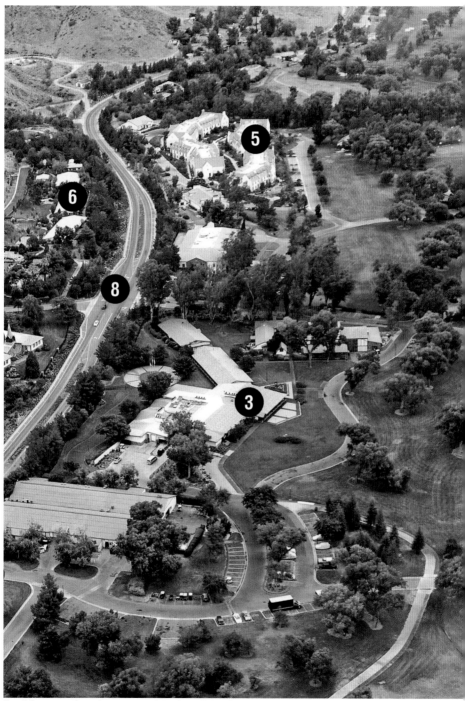

lived from 2006 until our escape. (6) The Villas, where David lives when he is at the base.
(7) David's office, colloquially called Building 50 after its number on a property usage plan.
(8) State Highway 79, which bisects the property. David has unsuccessfully tried to have the highway
closed several times. (9) The west gate through which Becky and I obtained our freedom on March
25, 2012.
Photo: Sinar Parman

*David's lavish 45,000 square foot office building,
which had to be rebuilt almost from scratch more than
once. Until I left, it was only used by David and his
personal office staff, which numbered about ten.
Photo: Sinar Parman*

mistake, because a dog came out of nowhere, grabbed the contents of the bag and began chowing down on a coffee cake, cellophane wrapper and all.

About my earlier reference to a "shore story": this was something developed on the *Apollo* that people on the ship would tell the locals ashore about who they were and what they were doing. It was called "telling an acceptable truth," which always boils down to a lie. If a Scientologist ever admits to using a shore story, it means he is lying, pure and simple.

For example, when the *Apollo* pulled into a new port, the shore story was that those aboard were either management consultants or trainees who were gaining experience before returning to their companies. Strictly speaking, that was true. The people onboard were managers—they were managing international Scientology. As well, students on board were learning Hubbard's latest developments in administrative technology, and some would eventually return to their organizations, though some also were recruited to join the Sea Org and so never made it home again.

When the Sea Org returned to land in Clearwater in 1975, Hubbard used a front group called Southern Land Developing and Leasing Corporation to buy the Fort Harrison Hotel for a tenant supposedly called United Churches of Florida. That was the shore story, in other words, a lie.

At any rate, a couple days after the funeral in Los Angeles, Ray Mithoff, then the most senior technically trained person in the church, came to me to give me "more information" about the event. He said that before Hubbard died, the two of them had been talking, and Hubbard had asked Ray if he thought people would miss him. Ray said probably so. Hubbard said they shouldn't, and at the end of their conversation he went into his room. A couple of hours later he was gone.

When someone tells you something that is true, it has the ring of truth to it. When something is only partially true, it has a different, somewhat hollow ring, and I knew even then that what Ray was telling me was bullshit. He had come to see me because Dave knew that I was gregarious and talked to a lot of people and that if I bought that story and passed it on, people would tend to accept it. I never bought it—or passed it on.

Another time I was up in David's office, which was located on the north side of the property overlooking the highway. We were discussing something or other, and while we were talking, the payroll person from David's organization, the Religious Technology Center, walked into the office and handed David his weekly pay in cash. Dave looked at it briefly, said, "Thanks," and the guy walked out. Dave laid the money on the desk and we continued our conversation. I could see the cash paper-clipped to the invoice, and it was the same allowance all staffers were receiving at the time, I think $30. (Room and board were provided by the Sea Org, of course.) I will bet you dollars to doughnuts that David staged that little interlude to get me to think that he was making the same as every other Sea Org member on the base. Again, he knew that I was gregarious and would tell people, "You know, COB, poor guy, he works so hard but only makes the same pay as the rest of us." I never did. (David holds the post of Chairman of the Board of the Religious Technology Center, and people refer to him as C-O-B.)

That March, at L. Ron Hubbard's annual birthday celebration two months after his death—a day that Scientology continues to celebrate as a holiday each year around his birthday—we released an album called *Road to Freedom* performed by "L. Ron Hubbard and Friends." We had 30 days to produce the entire album, which was impossible, as anybody in the music business would confirm. Yet, on day 30 at 8:30 in the morning, two guys drove off the base to LA to make masters. It was conceived, written, arranged, recorded and mixed in one month. We got no sleep for that month. David had demanded that the goal be met, and it was up to everyone else to do or die. We did but nearly died in the process.

Immediate arrangements were made with Scientology celebrities to contribute to the album. Since most were already in Los Angeles, it was only a matter of securing their agreement and then arranging for them to come to the base for their part of the production. These artists were there only when their parts were being recorded, of course. While they worked long hours when needed, they were spared the round-the-clock work put in by Sea Org members.

Despite everything, I thoroughly enjoyed working with John Travolta; Julia McGinnis Johnson, the opera and cabaret singer; Chick Corea; David Campbell; Amanda Ambrose, the famed jazz singer; Michael Roberts; Frank Stallone and other Scientology artists who came up to contribute to the effort.

John was a wonderful person to work with. After we finished recording one of his songs for the album, I gave him a ride back to Los Angeles and we had a nice conversation about nothing in particular. He used to call me Pops, because I played trumpet, as did Louis Armstrong, and that was one of his nicknames.

Frank, of course, is the younger brother of Sylvester Stallone. Frank was not a Scientologist, nor was Sly, but Frank had come to Portland to help with the protest in 1985. He was willing to contribute to the album and so came on board.

Julia McGinnis Johnson was another fabulous artist. What a voice. As a kid she was in the Sea Org and was one of L. Ron Hubbard's stewards aboard the *Apollo,* but she decided she was going to become famous as a singer, and she left and did it. She has since had a long and

successful career, mostly in Europe, as a mezzo-soprano in musical the-
ater. In 1984, she starred in the film *Carmen.*

The truth is that everyone on that project was great to work with.
People pitched in because they wanted to honor L. Ron Hubbard.
The album was wonderfully received by Scientologists when released
that March, the first such event after Hubbard's death, which made it
significant.

Working with great people and creating good products helped me
overlook the living conditions at the base because we all were there to
help make a better world. It wasn't horrible, but life in the Sea Org was
no country club. I lived in a house on the property with some of the
other single guys in the music department. Occasionally, every couple of
weeks or so, I took a day of liberty, as it was called, and did whatever I
wanted. In my early years, I took a vacation for a week or two each year.
Christmas holidays were nice, with a few days off and a lot of group
activities, great food, shows that we musicians put on, movies and just
relaxing with everybody on the base. Conditions, in other words, were
tolerable.

A tremendous number of diverse activities occurred on the base in
those days. Golden Era Productions was charged with producing all the
media for dissemination: training films; videos for PR purposes; Hubbard's lectures, not only in English but translated and recorded by voice
talent in a variety of languages; occasional updates of Hubbard's books.
In addition, the base facilities needed to be maintained and expanded,
and the management units with offices there needed to be supplied with
meals, housing and other services. This required a large and multifac-
eted organization with many specialized units. People trained for their
specialty and spent their days contributing to the overall effort. Since
I worked in the music department, I spent my days composing and arranging music that could be used in film or video productions.

By this time, my daughters, Denise and Lori, had married, and I was now a grandfather. Denise's husband was a Scientologist, but Lori's never became more involved than taking some introductory courses. That was never an issue one way or the other. I visited them while on leave when they all were living in New Hampshire, and I truly enjoyed my grand-kids. I would take them out in the woods because that was something I enjoyed as a kid. I taught them basic camping skills, such as how to build a fire, even in the rain—where to find dry wood, how to light it, that kind of thing. I taught them how to throw potatoes in the fire, cook hotdogs, common things that a granddad can show the young 'uns.

In 1988, the church held the maiden voyage for its new cruise ship, the *Freewinds*. It was a huge event because, on that first voyage from its home port in Curaçao, they released the most advanced of the Scientol-ogy auditing levels, which is delivered only aboard the ship. From 1950 until the end of his life, Hubbard more or less continuously released new developments in Dianetics and Scientology. One of the last of these was an advanced auditing course that he said should be delivered off the crossroads of the world, in other words, in a distraction-free environ-ment. The world had been out of his hair for most of the time he'd been at sea, and Scientology returned to sea with the *Freewinds*.

Before we got to the launch, we musicians had been up for days preparing music for the videos that would be shown during the week of events. We arrived dog tired, but instead of sleeping we were put to work, along with others, building the event stage. That was only the beginning. On that maiden voyage, the passengers, who were mostly high-roller Scientologists and celebrities, went to heaven; the rank-and-file Sea Org members went to hell. I had posh berthing—a deck chair in one of the offices. Other guys slept on the deck with a blanket.

For one gig we worked outdoors in the Caribbean heat until the moment we had to go to the venue for a sound check. We were sweating like pigs, went to the site, did the sound check and headed back to the ship with just enough time to change into our stage outfits—no time to shower—and do the show. It was BO City.

One thing to understand about the Sea Org: Hubbard and then David could sit in an office and think up groovy ideas to advance Scientology. Whether the resources to implement those ideas exist is another matter. Usually sufficient resources are not available to do things comfortably, so they get done uncomfortably. Often, because of rushed planning or slipshod execution, they have to be done over again a time or two or even more. Sea Org members become cynical after a few of these painful experiences and adopt the unwritten motto of the Sea Org: "There is never time to do it right but always time to do it twice."

Every year after 1988 Scientology held another anniversary cruise, and every year it was the same thing: stay up night after night to get everything ready, fly down to the ship and stay up night after night doing shows during the cruise. Everything was done to impress influential Scientologists and to make David and management look good. (As the years went on, management faded from the equation; more on that later.)

Each year the ship sailed to different ports in the Caribbean, and one year it sailed to Mexico. The musicians and some other staff members were going through immigration as a group, and four Mexican police were acting as gatekeepers. They spoke no English and we spoke no Spanish. I tried to explain that we were coming to play music. They shook their heads no. They weren't going to let us into the country. This could have become a real disaster but I got an idea. "Guys, get out your horns," I said to the others.

One guy took out his trombone, the next guy grabbed his clarinet and I took out my trumpet, and we played "Limehouse Blues." If you know the song, it is very up-tempo and jazzy. A couple times I looked at the head guard and winked, and he winked back at me. They were smiling and tapping their feet to the tune, and when we finished they applauded and gave us a thumbs-up. We got through immigration by playing "Limehouse Blues."

One of the most wonderful people I met during these yearly cruises was Isaac Hayes, who had become involved in Scientology in the mid-1990s. Beyond his iconic stature in the music world and popular culture, Isaac was a person of great courage. During the civil rights era, Isaac was the first African American to go into a Walgreen's in Memphis, Tennessee, in protest of the Jim Crow laws. Although he was a superstar when I met him, I found him to be a down-to-earth person and extremely humble.

I remember sitting in his cabin sharing stories about our youth. Isaac came from a poor family, and when his high school class sold chocolate bars to raise money for their activities, Isaac lived on the chocolate bars for an entire month. Later, when he became famous and had money, he repaid the school for the bars. That is the kind of person he was.

I told him about buying the Charles Atlas bodybuilding course when I was a kid. I had enough money for the down payment but could not afford to keep up with the monthly installments. I began receiving letters from the Atlas Company demanding payment, and I was sure that any day I would be dragged off to jail. Finally, I hit on an idea to get them off my back. I wrote a letter directly to Charles Atlas himself saying that I should not have to pay for the course because my chest muscles were always sore from the exercises. Isaac could not stop laughing at that one.

I once heard Isaac express his reason for being involved in Scientology: he wanted to help make a better world because he knew he was going to come back to it one day and wanted it to be a good place. Truly, Isaac was one of the nicest people I have ever known.

Notwithstanding that chewing-out I received at St. Hill, I have to say that my dealings with David were not bad during my early years at Gold, especially compared to later times. He had taken on the duty of giving final okay for many of the products that units on the base produced, and these included music scores for films, PR events and so on. I often brought music submissions up to his office and went over them with him, and we got along well. Though he was now the leader of the church, he was still friendly with me, though our interactions became more formal and businesslike.

One time he told me, "We don't believe in nepotism. The fact you're my father doesn't cut any ice around here." I accepted that.

After all, I was pretty proud of him for all the things he had achieved. I would overlook some things and forgive a lot of things that maybe I shouldn't have. I have a hard time playing the victim, and a lot of stuff just went by me with a "que sera" attitude. An example might be his rejecting a piece of music I had arranged. "Jesus Christ, this is a piece of crap!" he would say. "What are you guys doing down there?" instead of "Okay, here is what I had in mind, and here is where I think you went off the rails."

A year or two after I joined, a talented musician named Peter Schless joined Gold. He had written the music for a big hit called "On the Wings of Love" (the lyrics were by Jeffrey Osborne, who recorded it), had played with the Allman Brothers and was an extremely competent professional. He and I worked together a lot over the years and produced a lot of music together.

It was not easy to gain approval from David for film music. At times we would bust our guts to create something that worked, often staying up all night to try to get it right. The first time I was faced with an all-nighter, I wondered aloud about the wisdom of trying to work when dog tired, and someone snapped at me, "If you don't like it, just go route out of the Sea Org!" I learned to stay up all night but always viewed it as a punishment rather than something noble. When you are tired, you cannot think straight, you make mistakes and usually create more trouble for yourself.

One time, Peter Schless and I stayed up for 84 hours straight, doing music for a video. We wrote the theme, arranged it and recorded all the parts so it was a finished piece that fit exactly with the video. Then we crashed into bed, exhausted. We were proud that we got it done, but it was completely nuts.

Any good times I had did not last, however; they do not last for anybody who is in David's orbit, as I have long since learned. In the mid-1980s, Gold built a state-of-the-art music recording studio. No expense was spared to make it as fine as any studio in the world. Walls were two feet thick to dampen any sound from the roadway a hundred yards to the south. The studio was set on rubber plugs to separate it from the earth, further dampening vibrations. Lexan panels in the studio enhanced the sound. The theory behind its construction was to make it absolutely dead, meaning there would be no reverberation whatsoever in the studio, but reverb could be added after recording to make the music sound better for the particular venue where it would be played. The Massenburg music mixing board was one of only four in the world. The studio also had conference rooms, facilities for visiting artists to use, a kitchen, you name it. It was really top of the line.

A completely dead recording studio, besides being a near impossibility to create, was also a flawed concept to begin with, so David ordered several major overhauls of the entire facility. By 1987, he was the undisputed leader of Scientology, and his influence permeated everything at the base and over time extended to the farthest reaches of Scientology internationally. These renovations often tied up large sections of the organization for weeks or months at a time as people worked around the clock, replanning, renovating and rewiring the whole place at a cost of hundreds of thousands of dollars, maybe even more. Each time was a worse nightmare than the previous effort.

The modus operandi of these "evolutions," as they were called, was "punishment drive," which means coercing cooperation through punishment or threats thereof. In truth, that is the way the Church of Scientology operates today, and that mentality exists solely because of David Miscavige.

Here's an example of the degree to which it became institutionalized. One of David's henchmen, for there is no other term for this person, once was briefing the music department on something that needed to be done. "If you don't get this done, here is what is going to happen to you," he said and proceeded to rattle off what awaited us for noncompliance.

"Okay," I interjected, "that's the punishment. What's the reward if we get it done?"

"The reward is you don't get punished," he said in all seriousness.

L. Ron Hubbard wrote in numerous policies that punishment drive does not and has never worked. When a worker continues to toil under the threat of punishment, what actually impels the worker is his own willingness. It has nothing to do with punishment or its threat. But punishment drive is the way the church operates today. Punishment is preferable to any other motivation in its eyes. "If he doesn't work, punish him. Put him on beans and rice." Hubbard once cut an offending person's rations to simple rice and beans, which he alleged provided a complete protein diet, yet it becomes awfully unappealing three times a day for days or weeks on end. David modified the concept of carrot and stick to "stick, first, last and always." I recall talking with him one time about how to inspire people to accomplish things, and he said, "I'll tell you how to get work done—kick their ass, man." In other words, dominate them. That flew in the face of my observations and experience with the vast majority of the people at Gold: they were willing to do just about anything to advance Scientology. They were the most willing people I ever met.

In the midst of this misery, which would in time become much worse, a bright spot made it all worthwhile for me in the long run. For a time, Gold did internal promotions that involved sending some of the Gold crew down to the Los Angeles organizations dressed as characters from the technical training films they produced. One of those films had an *Alice in Wonderland* theme, so people dressed up as the Mad Hatter, the Queen of Hearts, and other characters and paraded around the organizations to drum up interest in the films. One character in particular caught my eye immediately: Alice, as played by Becky Bigelow, the daughter of Tom Bigelow, the racecar driver. Becky grew up around racetracks, from midget cars in Wisconsin to the speedway at Indianapolis, where Tom ran nine times, and I soon figured out excuses to discuss business with her seniors in the marketing area where Becky worked. To my everlasting joy, my interest in her was reciprocated, and we have never looked back.

I can now state unequivocally that I have experienced marriage from both ends of the spectrum. As stressful and traumatic as my marriage to Loretta was, my marriage to Becky has been really, really wonderful, better than I could have imagined. In 25 years of marriage, I can count the number of serious arguments we have had on one hand, literally. That was a week of life with Loretta. I say that only to make the point that people who want different things from life, as Loretta and I did, have the deck stacked against them in a big way. A mongoose and a cobra should never be married. When I think about what Loretta and I put each other through, with the arguments and the fights and my striking her, it seems like another lifetime. I don't think I would even be capable of considering something like that now. If you are fortunate to have a wonderful relationship with someone, like I have with Becky, here's my advice: cherish it with everything you've got.

Becky and I were granted a weekend off, just the two of us, and were married in Las Vegas in June 1990. Neither David nor any of my other kids or Becky's family attended. David used to joke with Becky about her being his stepmom, and he accepted the fact of our marriage. It is a good thing we wed when we did because things were about to go steeply downhill for Gold. By the next month, our chances of getting hitched would have been zero for a long, long time.

On August 10, 1990, a torrential storm hit the Hemet Valley. It poured and poured, causing mudslides across State Route 79, the road that bisects the base. Meteorologists termed it a 100-year event. There were flash floods throughout the Hemet Valley, one of which caused water damage to some buildings on the base, including David's own quarters. A drain in front of his room clogged, and water seeped under the door, soaking the carpet. His secretary had to unblock the drain herself since everyone else was out dealing with the damage at the highway.

After dinner that evening, David ordered the entire base to muster in the dining area, which was the only space large enough to accommodate everyone. He ordered the Gold staff to stand at the front, and he lashed out at us for half an hour, maybe even longer, ranting about how the damage was entirely our fault. He could brutalize a single individual verbally, which we all knew because nearly everyone had either experienced it personally or seen it done to others. On this occasion, though, he ramped up his intensity to a level none of us had seen before.

The next day, the entirety of Gold was subjected to draconian measures undoubtedly thought up by David himself. Because Gold was tasked with the maintenance and security of the base, he blamed the organization for what had happened. All privileges were revoked, every

Gold staff member was assigned a condition of Confusion (meaning that our status as a group was considered well below zero), and we were forced to take part in a "boot camp" that was a travesty of the concept. It consisted of being dressed down regularly as a group by more of David's henchmen and marching around the base for hours on end. As someone who went through Marine boot camp and came out the other side a capable Marine, I can say that David's version was intended solely to nullify people, not to make them more competent. The whole crew was mustered up several times a day, and if anyone was late to a muster, the penalty was that the offending person had to stay up all that night working on some mundane task and go without sleep.

Frankly, after that flood, life in the Sea Org became a downward spiral. Almost nothing we musicians did was considered worthy of approval. Eventually, the music department had to use classic rock songs in videos because we could not get a melody approved.

And this became a bad scene indeed when almost the entire base was mired in what we called "event mode," which in short order became a runaway freight train.

FOURTEEN

FRANKENSTEIN'S MONSTER

N LATE SUMMER 1984, AS PART OF THE CHURCH'S STRATEGY to fund ongoing litigation, of which there was much at the time, someone came up with the idea of forming the International Association of Scientologists (IAS), a membership organization that all Scientologists had to join to receive church services. Several years earlier, after the FBI raided the church and numerous staff, including Mary Sue Hubbard, were facing prison terms, the church had established a legal defense fund that brought in a considerable amount of money. The new idea behind IAS was to repackage that fund to create a new source of income. Attorneys explained how it could be set up offshore to put it beyond the reach of the IRS or an agency of any government. Six weeks later, in October, church leaders, including David, gathered at St. Hill to sign a Pledge to Mankind to support the Aims of Scientology. The event, which signified the formation of the IAS, was videotaped and then played to Scientologists all over the world. The video proved hugely popular, but it marked the birth of a Frankenstein's monster.

That first event soon spawned others: a New Year's celebration, an LRH birthday celebration, a May 9 Dianetics anniversary, a weeklong *Freewinds* Maiden Voyage Anniversary celebration, an Auditor's Day celebration and, coming full circle, an IAS celebration every October. As time went on, another event, held at the church's Celebrity Centre in Hollywood, a study center and hotel for stars, was added to the roster. Year after year these events became more lavish, with elaborate stage decorations, specially produced videos to announce the latest church accomplishment or product for sale, graphic effects to highlight church expansion, all intended to increase the impact of speeches that church executives and, increasingly, David himself delivered by teleprompter.

To prepare for the productions, people were pulled away from their usual duties and sucked into frantic event-related activities. The shows became base-wide nightmares, although I must admit they did accomplish the only effect David truly wanted: Scientology audiences deeply impressed with Scientology's ever-widening impact on society under his leadership. The events became showcases for such things as Scientology's disaster relief efforts, its antidrug campaigns, and its continual push, as spearheaded by David, to make a better world through the works of L. Ron Hubbard.

The reality is, however, that these extravaganzas were Scientology's Potemkin villages. Just as Russian military leader Grigory Potemkin built fake villages to impress Catherine the Great during a tour of Crimea, David erected hollow facades of Scientology expansion and good works to amaze Scientologists. Many, if not most, of the nifty programs (for example, a new broadcast television advertising campaign "that will reach billions with the message of Scientology") announced at events were never completed. The busy churches around the world featured in specially prepared videos were filled with parishioners who had been press-ganged into creating the appearance of a hive of activity, which disappeared the minute the video crew left town.

The agenda behind these events became plain after some time: they were more to cement David's position as leader of the church than to highlight any accomplishments of Scientology itself. In recent years, both aspects have become blurred entirely. Each evolution of an event was stressful for David, and his frustration levels ratcheted up as deadlines for completion of various aspects of the production came and went. For him, however, the night of the show always provided a big payoff in terms of ego boost when adoring audiences showered him with thundering ovations. As the years rolled on, the reward for anybody working on an event was simply a night's sleep.

Preparation for an event involved nearly the entire base population of several hundred for weeks and weeks, often around the clock. Pulling off one of these events requires a tremendous amount of work:

- Management executives have to plan the event;
- researchers need to gather the news and information needed for the speechwriters, who must write the speeches and scripts for videos to be shown at the event;
- compilations people have to prepare the books, courses or materials to be presented;
- the film and video department must shoot the required videos and prepare the graphics shown during the event;
- the editing department has to edit everything;
- the musicians must compose, record and mix all the music;
- construction crews have to build the ornate stage decorations;
- logistics personnel need to pack up and transport everything to the venue, usually in Los Angeles, Clearwater, St. Hill or on the *Freewinds*;

- marketing people must prepare promotional materials;
- executives in charge of various sectors of the Scientology network have to write programs that their people at lower echelons must execute for the event; and
- base support personnel must perform all their usual services but on wildly extended schedules.

David directly manages virtually every aspect of these activities. He stirs the soup, and nothing advances to the next stage until he gives his approval. When I was involved, the usual result, which I am sure continues to this day, was that several months of production had to be compressed into a few weeks. The stress level at these times is hard to describe. Almost without exception, David was unhappy with the initial planning, speeches, videos, editing, music or the promotion. He gave no thought to deadlines or to how each step of the work depended on previous steps by other units—the musicians, for instance, could not begin their job until David had approved the video edits. In the music department, we would do as much as we could beforehand, but mostly we had to mark time until David gave his final blessing, which was usually just days before the show. Then it would be a total madhouse, day and night, until we were done. When everything was "in the can," the relief throughout the base was palpable because people couldn't wait to fall into bed.

I haven't looked up the word *micromanagement* in a dictionary recently, but I am convinced that if I did, I would find David's picture next to the definition. He micromanaged every aspect of every event, often complaining loudly that he had to do it because everyone else working on the event was incompetent.

Music was an integral part of each show, from opening themes to music that accompanied videos and sometimes live performances, particularly aboard the *Freewinds,* which had a week of nightly events each June.

The entire international base at Gold revolved around these events. One event ended and preparations for the next began. The music department suffered this nightmare seven times a year. Remember, we had to wait until the videos were okayed. The usual routine was that the people working on the videos stayed awake around the clock, shooting and reshooting, editing and reediting these videos to the last minute; when the final edit came to us, we had no time to do the music. It went on like this for nearly every single event, and that's no exaggeration. We were up day and night scoring, recording, mixing and then seeking approval from David's office.

For the *Freewinds* cruises, we also prepared different shows for most nights of the voyage. Unless you have worked on an event in the Sea Org at Gold, you haven't lived. Let me correct that: you haven't lived a nightmare.

Often, the stress levels ratcheted up even higher, thanks to various executives who had adopted David's methods of dealing with people. You could call it the "monkey see, monkey do" theory of executive training. It wasn't everybody who behaved like that, but those who eschewed that sort of behavior did not last too long, as I remember. One executive who did adopt David's "management style" often dealt with the music area. He has long since tired of David and is no longer in the Sea Org. While he was there and having to answer to David, though, he mimicked some of David's people-handling tactics.

One time, this executive came into the music area to check on the progress of a piece we were working on. Peter Schless and I were at the keyboard when the executive walked in with an arrogant sneer on his face and said, "Boy, you guys are really something. I could go upstairs on my shitty little keyboard, and 20 minutes later I could give you a piece that would blow away the shit that you guys do. Feh!" and walked out of the room in disgust.

So, added to the compressed deadlines to get something done, on top of little or no sleep, we had to deal with stuff like that. And this was going on all over the base as each area was working on its own part of the event.

This executive later demonstrated to all of us in music that his arrogance about his knowledge of music was nothing more than a facade. He prided himself on having acute listening skills that could determine what was right and what was wrong with a piece of music or a mix. His confidence in his ability in this area was supreme.

One day he was supervising us as we did a mix. He stood there listening intently, rubbing his chin wisely. A technician sat at the equalizer, a machine you can use to strengthen or weaken the sound frequencies at specific points. The idea is to get a good balance of all the low notes and high notes so everything blends together pleasantly, and an equalizer helps you do that.

"Give me one more tick at 250," he said knowingly. That meant he wanted to slightly raise the volume at 250 vibrations a second. The technician did so.

"Okay, give me a tick at 5K," he said, by which he meant the technician should make the sound level at 5,000 vibrations a little louder.

He listened a little longer. "Okay, take off the tick at 250." He listened a little longer. "Okay. Perfect. It's approved," he announced and walked out, secure in his place in the universe, shoulders back and head held high.

Well, good. Glad that is done, we all thought, as we began to note down the settings that were part of the record-keeping protocol for any piece of music. Only then did we notice that the equalizer had not been turned on.

Talk about the emperor's new clothes. We had a real good laugh at his expense and adjusted our attitudes toward him forever.

Among all this misery, what kept us there was our goal to make the world a better place and help mankind. The pressures and the punishment-driven management methods only blunted people's resolve, and their use became more frequent as time went on.

Of course, no one who considers joining the Sea Org is ever told what happens after you sign your billion-year contract. Can you imagine someone joining the Sea Org to go to Gold as I did and being told the truth by their recruiter? "Okay, you've decided to join the Sea Org. Congratulations and welcome. We're glad to have you as part of the team. Now, uh, chances are you aren't going to get any time for study or Scientology services or to do anything other than your job, because that's all that counts. You're going to get substandard food. The galley crew will do its best to prepare it in a way that is palatable and somewhat nutritious, but at one point the food allocation for a Gold staff member will be three dollars per person per day. Your incoming mail will be opened and read before you get it. The mail you send out will be read before it goes out. Any phone call you make will be monitored by a person listening on an extension. You will not be allowed to leave the base to go shopping at a store. If you have to see a doctor, you must have an escort—in other words, a guard—so you don't leave. Your everyday activity will be monitored minutely, and there will come a point where you will not have had a regular day off for years. This is how your life will be from this day forward. Sign here."

It wasn't like that when I joined the Sea Org. How does it get to that point? By tiny increments. A small change here, a small change there. A slight modification of a rule here, another one there. You agree to each one because it seems like no great loss of liberty or freedom of movement or of thought. It is for the greater good, you rationalize. The next thing you know, you can't even go into town to buy Christmas presents to mail to the family you have not seen in ten years. That's how you arrive in the position I just described.

How you get any group of people—a small group, a large group, a whole country—to become trapped is by their own state of mind and their own consent to be trapped. They have to be willing to be there and be trapped.

"Look," the explanation begins, "there are people off the base causing us trouble so we need to start checking all the letters that go out. It's for your own good and the safety of the base."

I'll tell you how this started. Around 1990 the marketing people had phones they could use to call vendors who produced the avalanche of promotion the church was sending out. One guy was using the phones to talk to his mother nearly every day and telling her about what was happening on the base, particularly as it related to Tom Cruise, who was there with Nicole Kidman. Both were doing courses and auditing at the base. The guy's mother was passing the information on to the *National Enquirer,* and you can imagine the explosion when that came to light.

Afterward, everybody had to request written authorization to call his or her family. Once that was granted, you could make your call, but somebody was always on an extension in another office, eavesdropping on everything being said. One Christmas Becky called her mother, who had been violently ill with the flu. She went on and on about her misery, all while one of the security personnel listened in. Can you imagine how mortified she would have been if she knew? Of course, the staff member placing the call cannot let on that this is happening, but you can imagine the strain it placed on the conversation. Ever since 1990, every time a Gold base staff member calls their family, that is what happens. That is the solution put in place to "solve" the problem of someone's feeding celebrity information to his mother long ago. That "solution" has caused so many more problems that it's ridiculous.

Personal mail brought another invasion of a staff member's privacy. You would write a letter to a family member or friend, address the envelope and put a stamp on it but leave the envelope unsealed. You would place it in the mail station in your work area where each person in that building had a basket for incoming mail, memos, magazines, and the like. The mail runner would collect any outgoing letters and send them to the security department, where a member of the security force would read the letter. If the letter was deemed okay, the envelope was sealed and sent out to be mailed. If it wasn't okay—if the security person objected to something you had written—the letter came back to you to fix before it could go out. During World War II, the government checked mail to ensure sensitive operations were not being compromised. That was exactly the mentality at the Gold base, yet the only enemies on the horizon were in somebody's mind.

The irony is that Scientology loudly trumpets its support of the United Nations' Universal Declaration of Human Rights; however, every staff member at the base was forced to sign away their rights to privacy. This really got to Becky because, working in marketing, she took part in creating church promotional magazines that contained the declaration in special issues every year. She once made a crack about the hypocrisy of the situation to her senior manager in marketing, and it created a brouhaha with a senior executive dressing her down in front of another group of executives and other staff, which, as it happened, included me.

That's how the craziness starts. People will respond to an authority figure. If someone has authority, people tend to listen to that person. Not just the Germans listening to Hitler but anybody listening to someone higher in the pecking order. So you agree to go to a muster four times a day, something you would never do if left to your own devices. You agree to have someone check your room to make sure it is clean. You agree to have your mail checked. You agree to have someone listen on an extension when you phone a family member. You agree to stay in an enclosed compound and not go to a store.

At the base, control was exerted over what a person could write and say, and this mania even extended to an attempt to control what a person had witnessed. Here is how that came about.

In the mid-1980s, Hubbard developed something he called the Truth Rundown in response to a comment a staff member had made on a survey. The gist of the comment was that Hubbard was difficult to work with on the set during the year he spent making technical training films. The person had been there for that whole year and experienced Hubbard's numerous blowups when things did not go according to his demands, and the writer expressed this in answering the survey.

Hubbard's response was to theorize that the man's observations were most likely a justification of or cover-up for harmful actions by the person himself. According to Hubbard, such criticisms of a well-intentioned person usually are found to be false or merely hearsay. The remedy was to take the individual into an auditing session and begin tracing *his* harmful actions and bring them to light. Now, here is where it gets creepy: the goal of this activity was to convince the person that what he thought he had seen (with his own eyes, mind you) was not what he actually had seen but merely his rationalization for his own less-than-stellar behavior. In other words, the perfect outcome of the Truth Rundown would be for someone to disavow what he or she had witnessed. Hubbard also wrote that the person should offer to address the group and, in an act of contrition, apologize for spreading false and misleading information about so-and-so and say, in essence, "It was just my own nasty secrets that made me say these things." To me, this sounded a lot like the *Manchurian Candidate,* though I will add that I cannot recall the rundown's ever achieving the successful outcome that Hubbard envisioned. People observe what they observe, and what I observed were increasing restrictions on my freedoms of thought and expression.

I once tried out my theory of incremental concessions with a taxi driver. Peter Schless and I were taking a taxi to a gig site in Mexico, where we'd docked during a Maiden Voyage Anniversary cruise.

I asked the driver, "Have you ever heard of the pyramids of Chichen Itza?"

"Oh, yes, very famous. I know them well," he replied.

"I wonder how they got there?" I said.

"I don't know," he answered.

"You know, I heard that even with modern-day technology, you couldn't move stones that big," I said. "Did you know that?"

"No, I didn't know that."

"Yeah, that's what I heard," I continued.

"Well, it's possible that that is true," he agreed. I got him to agree to that one point.

After continuing to get a slight agreement here and a slight agreement there, we arrived at the gig site, and I asked the driver, "Okay, then, who built the pyramids at Chichen Itza?"

"People from outer space," he replied.

I had proved to myself that my theory worked, and I had a witness. Peter laughed his ass off when we got out of the taxi.

That is a humorous example, but life in the Sea Org was not a joke. At one point in the early 2000s, I told Becky, "I cannot go on living like this." She agreed.

As we were walking to lunch one day, I said to one of the guys in the music area, "I have no intention of living the rest of my life like this."

He turned to me and said, "Ronnie, why don't you tell COB? Do you ever talk to him? Tell him how bad it is."

A lot of good that would have done. David was the one who made it that way! In the Marines, when you are down in the trenches and everything is going to hell around you, you don't look sideways, you look up the chain of command. Because of that, I knew that David was responsible.

Yet his recognition of his responsibility for creating the terrible conditions at the base was exactly zero. I offer this example: one day I was talking with Marc Yager, one of the top church executives for many years and thus one of David's favorite punching bags. At one point, Marc mentioned to me that he had remarked to David, "Some people in Gold have not had a liberty in 12 years." According to Mark, David's response was utter surprise. "That's insane," he said, thereby pretending that he had no hand in it while being the sole creator of the arbitrary rules that led to the conditions where people could go for that long without a day off.

David had closely aligned himself with L. Ron Hubbard. When LRH died, some people thought that Hubbard had appointed David as his successor, which I am certain is not true. Here is why I think so: Throughout his life, Hubbard wrote down nearly everything in longhand, including the vast majority of the thousands of church policies and technical bulletins he wrote. He even wrote whole books in longhand. He recorded thousands of public lectures and thousands more briefings of executives. He kept a small cassette recorder next to his bed in case an idea came to him in the middle of the night. Yet he said not a word about arguably the most important decision of his life—who should carry on his life's work. My opinion is that Hubbard left no plan for succession. Here was a man who wrote everything down. He couldn't have scrawled a note on his deathbed that said, "I hereby appoint David Miscavige as my successor"?

During his time in the Sea Org, however, David had wormed his way into a position that made him the gatekeeper for communications to and from Hubbard. That gave David immense authority. Because he had that authority, people would listen to him, which is another definition of power, something David told me as well as others. "Power is when people will listen to you," as he put it. Knowing this, he used that authority to make people do things they would not normally do. In the Sea Org, people assume that any orders come from COB, so they follow them. It is that simple.

I saw him ruthlessly take people apart with a withering glare and high-decibel, profanity-laced accusations. You did not want to cross him. His modus operandi was domination through nullification. You might walk into another area of the org—say, editing—and there he would be, ripping somebody apart. A different area on another day, same thing. You were glad it was not happening to you. A corporate management style popular up until the 1980s was the tough boss who yells at employees. It has long since gone out of favor, but it is the palest approximation of the way David has run the church since he took over.

Every staff member was, more often than not, in a rattled condition all of the time. The facility at Gold had a large CD production plant, built at great expense just as CDs were being replaced by digital downloads. Quite often we were called to all-hands work details to stuff lecture CDs into their cases so they could be shrink-wrapped and sent out. The thousands and thousands of CDs coming off the line were far more than the staff posted in the area could deal with, so the rest of the org would be called in for half an hour after lunch, for example. One day Becky and I were standing next to each other while we stuffed CDs when David arrived for an inspection and noticed us. A person in his entourage came over and told Becky she had to move because it was not "personal time." Anything to make your life more miserable.

Much of what I have written in this chapter is bad enough, but the worst thing is this: I am actually telling the truth.

It gets even worse, however, but before I dive into that I have a piece of advice:

Do not ever sign away any right you have as an individual.

Don't ever sign anything that will allow someone to read your mail or listen to your phone calls or restrict your freedom of movement. If you do, you have allowed the erosion of freedoms that I consider your birthright; you will have started to fashion the key that fits the lock of the mental prison you will find yourself in, and you do not own that key. That's how it starts, so do not do it. If you find yourself in a relationship with another person, group or institution that begins to try to take away some of your rights, and the situation is too big for you to deal with head-on, find a side door and get out. Once you are in a safer position, you can take action to disempower that person or group.

FIFTEEN

THE HOLE

FOR YEARS, LIFE BUMPED ALONG RELATIVELY UNPLEASANTLY as I have described, until the beginning of 2004 when David instituted something that later became infamous as "the Hole." Stories abound on the Internet about the abuses that occurred in the Hole, but no one, to my knowledge, has come forward with the rationale, if you can call it that, for its formation.

Around 1979, L. Ron Hubbard determined that lack of proper marketing was the reason for the disappointing expansion of Scientology. He began a study of marketing texts and wrote numerous policy letters about marketing as it relates to Scientology. He ordered the establishment of a sizable marketing unit. He also decreed that if the management of Scientology ever dismantled marketing, the managerial arm itself was to be shut down and reconstructed.

David used that order as a pretense to shut down management and confine executives to their offices, which at the time consisted of a pair of double-wide renovated trailers that had conference rooms, offices and cubicles where management executives worked. At one point, iron bars were placed over windows, and a guard stood outside the only exit 24 hours a day. International management executives along with executives from Gold, as well as other staff members David believed were a drag on his time and attention, were thrown into this purgatory. According to multiple accounts, people were not permitted to leave. While they were not particularly cramped for space, the conditions in the Hole were miserable. People who were there have told me that they slept on the floor under desks or in offices in sleeping bags. Once a day they were marched down to the estates' maintenance building for a shower. They ate leftovers from the galley. Debbie Cook, a former Scientology executive, testified in a lawsuit that David had the air-conditioning turned off as punishment during a two-week stretch in the summer of 2007 when temperatures reached over 100 degrees. After Cook's testimony, the church issued a statement saying that Cook was "clearly bitter and falsely vilifying the religion she once was a part of."

The daily activities of people in the Hole consisted of either writing down or verbally confessing their sins. Ostensibly, they were following Hubbard's protocol to get back into good graces within the group and Scientology in general. That procedure contained a series of steps one had to follow after having been declared a "suppressive person," in other words, someone dedicated to the destruction of Scientology. That this would even be considered possible among the group of people who were inarguably the most dedicated Scientologists in the world tells you immediately how screwball the whole affair was. Despite the accounts of former members who experienced it firsthand, the church, in the person of a lawyer who was not under oath, put out a statement denying that the Hole ever existed.

According to those who were in the Hole, the routine of people sitting in a room and writing page after page of their transgressions day after day later devolved into each of these people standing before the other restricted personnel and confessing their misdeeds or evil intentions. As described by Mike Rinder, a former top executive in the church, and other former Sea Org members, these group confessions were often brutal affairs. One person was directed to stand in front of the group (all told there must have been about 100 people in the Hole at various times) and confess the ways in which he or she had been ineffective on the job, hampered the expansion of Scientology and, worst of all, sabotage all the work David was doing to salvage Scientology (from who or what was never made clear). People formerly confined to the Hole say that if they failed to confess or their confessions were deemed disingenuous, the person was screamed at and often slapped, pushed and punched by other persons held there. Per published accounts, this went on for weeks, which turned into months, and some executives spent five to seven years locked up there. The church denies that David has fostered a management culture that encourages physical abuse and says that when he learned that executives were physically abusing staff members, he put a stop to it and demoted the perpetrators.

One day I came out of the music rehearsal building, which was just a stone's throw from where all this insanity was going on. Outside the trailers was a large U-Haul truck, just sitting there. Hmm, I speculated, they must be getting rid of some old furniture or maybe buying new stuff. Maybe some stuff has to be moved from the other side of the property. I had no idea what that truck was doing there, but two days later it was gone, and I only recently found out why it was there. It was another cruel ruse cooked up by David to further nullify the people in the Hole. People at Gold had no idea what was going on inside the building at the time—and if anybody did know, they weren't talking.

Here is what multiple people who were involved told me and the press: One evening, David came down to the Hole from his office

carrying a boom box. He announced to the captives that he was going to show them what their inactivity, incompetence and evil intentions were doing to the rest of humanity. He said they were going to
play a game of musical chairs, and the song he had selected to play was
Queen's "Bohemian Rhapsody," the lyrics to which include this famous
line, just to drive the point home: "Nothing really matters to me."

He further explained that anyone put out of the game would be
banished from the base. They would be reposted to a small and failing
church somewhere in a far corner of the globe. They would be separated from their spouse or other family members. Again, at the time,
the people at Gold had no idea this had occurred, but I have been told
it was traumatic for many. The U-Haul sitting outside was to be used
to gather people's belongings. He had plane tickets booked to the far
corners of the Scientology world: Australia, Africa, New Zealand. He
made the threat very, very real. I have spoken to people who were forced
to participate, and the stories are not pleasant. They say no one dared to
call David on the charade he was enacting, and people played the game
for blood. Clothes were torn, people were thrown around, chairs were
broken. The most insane thing about it was that people were actually
fighting to stay! In the end nobody was sent away. The next day people
were left wondering when they would be moved off the base, but after
a day or two they began to realize the whole thing had been nothing
more than a threat and a demonstration of the cruelty of which David
was capable. The church told the *Tampa Bay Times* that the accounts of
the musical chairs game by Mike Rinder and other former executives
are overblown. The church claims that David was just trying to make
a point about how personnel transfers are like "musical chairs" and can
harm a group's progress.

My wife, Becky, once heard David tell a church employee being considered for promotion that Hubbard had instructed David to

disband and re-form management if marketing ceased to be an important priority. As I said, David's justification for starting the Hole was that marketing had shrunk beyond an irreducible minimum. Yet the flaw in his reasoning is illustrated by his not having followed the second part of Hubbard's order: to reconstruct management. To this day, so far as I know, no international management structure has been re-formed with executives authorized to run assigned areas. In fact, the overall structure of base organizations was thrown into confusion at about the time the Hole was created, with different units merged then separated, and then merged again; organizations were moved to one building, then back to their earlier location. Mass confusion was the order of the day, a day that lasted for years and, for all I know, might still be going on.

What's more, the person who dismantled marketing was David himself. My wife and close friends who worked in marketing tell me that with unrealistic time expectations, capricious rejections, changing his mind about broad strategies that were not communicated clearly but only tossed off in passing—"Oh, and by the way that plan X has to change"—as well as through micromanaging every aspect of most marketing work, people had no real option other than to leave the area, either by escaping (called "blowing") or being relieved of one's duties (being "busted"). So marketing dwindled. Per the organizational structure, there should have been at least half a dozen layers of management between the marketing staff and David, yet requests for marketing decisions went directly to him, and anyone in between was reduced to a rubber stamp, catching hell if they failed to submit paperwork to David on time. David always wanted things *now!* In that sense he is not unlike the three-year-old who sees something and wants it immediately, except that David has the unlimited and unquestioned authority to demand it.

Becky worked in the marketing area for years and told me what life was like there. Some of the things David did with marketing give insight into the way he has mismanaged Scientology all over the world. Over time, the number of people in marketing had dwindled. Many of the departures were, you guessed it, the direct result of one of David's meddlesome, spur-of-the-moment orders. Then, six months later, he would find out how few people were left in marketing (often because of the insanely executed increase in personnel in another area), and he would pronounce himself shocked at the state of the area. He would go on a campaign to immediately bolster the marketing staff, and that, of course, necessitated taking personnel from another area, with the result that those areas now were becoming understaffed. This kind of "du jour" management style, capriciously focusing on one area this week and another area next week, kept the organization in a general state of turmoil, as you can imagine. The only stable thing about the organization at the base was its instability.

David had a way of doing the same thing with individual staffers. Someone who was doing well on the job would come into favor with David. The staff member would be held up as an example of someone who was effective, productive and, most important, getting things done that COB wanted done. The object of this adulation naturally began to feel pretty good, especially in light of the general attitude toward most staff members, either that they were nobodies or people who were, in David's words, actively sabotaging what he was trying to accomplish. Since COB had made himself the unquestioned authority for all of Scientology, word that someone had received praise or acknowledgment from him spread quickly through the ranks, and that person quickly became known as being in David's good graces. What usually followed was a promotion to a position with greater responsibility because David was always on the lookout for people he thought might be able to help him manage some area of Scientology so he would not be saddled with "doing everything myself," his most common refrain. Oftentimes, his latest "golden child" came from an organization that was lower than Gold in the Scientology hierarchy and was brought to the international headquarters at Gold. David would, of course, have briefed the anointed one on what he, David, thought of the organizations and units on the base and instilled his attitudes in his new favorite; these attitudes were invariably negative about everything at the base, so the new executive would be disaffected from the outset.

It became fairly predictable that within six months, or a year at most, the golden child would fall out of favor and be removed from the job or even relegated to the Hole with the rest of management. This scenario was repeated often enough that the more hardened base staff would see a new executive as part of David's entourage and say under their breath, "Enjoy the honeymoon while it lasts, sucker."

The result of such treatment was that the people around David spent their lives roller-skating on bongo boards—they were constantly off balance. David had ways of keeping people off kilter. He might go into a meeting about, say, a marketing submission, and in attendance would be not only people from marketing but also executives in charge of marketing and even the senior executives for that area. Now, these other executives also had other areas of responsibility in addition to marketing. David might walk into the meeting and fire off pointed questions at one of the attending execs about something that was "flapping" (an unexpected emergency that is not being handled) in another part of that person's job. He might tear into the executive about the flap for a minute or two before getting down to the actual business of the meeting. The person who received the dressing down would leave the meeting completely rattled, but others who had been present also felt destabilized because they knew well that they could have been singled out. As a highly energetic micromanager, David knew just about everything of importance that was happening on the base, often more than the executive whose area it was, and you could see he took a measure of satisfaction in informing others of something flapping in a certain area.

He wore mirrored sunglasses, the kind that hide the eyes, which made it difficult to read whether some remark he made was a joke or serious. He took obvious pleasure in keeping others guessing about what he meant by a statement he had made. He could say something in jest to someone who did not know how to take it and that person would then be hit with a sharp "Why aren't you laughing?" It worked both ways. Someone might say something humorous, and you could not tell how he took it because you could not see his eyes. The worst thing of all was when you thought he was joking and laughed when he was serious. Then you were done for. "What the hell is so goddamned funny?!" Gulp.

Another technique he used was to brief the base and use the occasion to denigrate a particular person or several people, depending on his mood, in front of the assembled staff. One leading executive, once a close friend of David's, became the subject of an entire briefing in which the executive's supposed attempts to "undercut and even overthrow Dave" (or so one witness told us) were laid out in detail for all to hear. The net result, of course, was to turn everybody on the base against the poor man. He was subsequently banished to live in a literal swamp on the base property for a year. He had to build his own lean-to out of bamboo and tarps and was restricted to a fenced-in area of maybe an acre.

The result of the way David ran things was that people generally felt their jobs were in danger or that wholesale changes might be made in their area at any time. As you would conclude, every area of the base that David was involved in was frantically busy while producing almost nothing of value except under extreme duress.

David used one other tactic, not just on marketing people but on nearly everyone on the base—sleep deprivation. It became a source of tremendous pain (but also a twisted sense of pride if you could manage to stay awake during the ordeal) for someone to go without sleep for days on end after David had issued an impossible-to-achieve deadline. That was the way he instigated the practice. He never expressly demanded that people go without sleep. He did, however, demand, time and again, that something "better be done by the time I come in in the morning," which of course meant staying up all night to complete the task. Often, meetings during which David issued the demand ran well into the evening, sometimes hours beyond what was necessary to communicate the order.

Well, as any fool knows, going without sleep makes it harder to think, which results in poor decisions and mistakes. Naturally, David, well rested and fed when he arrived at work the following day, would spot the typos or poorly thought-out proposal, blow a gasket and send the submission back in flames; then the whole thing would begin again, resulting in even more mistakes. Meanwhile, people went without sleep. The situation became chronic for some staff members, and it was not unusual for people to exist for months on a few hours of sleep a night, rarely seeing their own beds and often sleeping at their desks or on the office carpet.

Sleep deprivation spread nearly base-wide around event time, when David's usual state of bad temper ramped up to new levels. His excuse was that he was surrounded by incompetents, and the only one he could count on to hold the line on quality was himself. Of course, demanding a standard of quality that is absolute or unobtainable is just another way to gum up the works and bring everything to a halt. I think David knew this and from time to time imposed these standards simply because he could. In his mind, everyone else who was working on the show was useless or, worse, out to sabotage the entire event. So, in addition to having to deal with the dead tiredness, lack of proper meals, no showers, no changes of clothes and a routine of coffee and cigarettes, people also were subjected to doses of invalidation and nullification dished out multiple times per day. It was nuts.

I was never thrown into the Hole, and neither was most of the Gold staff; nevertheless, the effects of the Hole seeped into the organization and made life even more distasteful, if that was possible. David engineered this by throwing some or all of the Gold executives into the Hole for a couple of weeks. When they were released, they were expected to take the lessons they had learned during their incarceration and apply them to the rest of Gold. And they did. There were frequent daily verbal and even physical fights among the general staff. Upbraiding people at musters and staff meetings became the standard mode of operation. What became known as "group seances" occurred at Gold—personnel responsible for areas that were "flapping" were forced to stand in front of the entire group and confess their sins, as was done in the Hole. The allusion to seances was sarcastic, since the purported purpose of these exercises was to create a magical change in the overall organization wherein Gold would suddenly become a cohesive, productive team overnight. I hope that I am communicating at least a whisper of the craziness of these times.

Nullification of junior staffers by senior staffers became the norm. At the weekly staff meetings or on random occasions, the staff was gathered and various people would be brought to the front and ordered to "tell the group what you are doing to sabotage COB's orders." If the person came up with something to satisfy the growing bloodlust, people would shout out, "What else did you do?" "When?" "Why?" and badger the person. At times, these group confessions were not dissimilar to descriptions in *Lord of the Flies*.

On Saturdays, the general schedule was a bit different than on weekdays. People were allowed out of their offices to work around the base, helping maintain the grounds or work on new construction projects. For most, it was the best day of the week. Being outdoors, getting some fresh air, learning to do something new was a joy compared to the rest of the week. People worked on renovations until dinner. In the evening there might be a base briefing from COB or the playing of one of Hubbard's lectures. All the units on the base attended; it was mandatory. RTC people were also there but not to enjoy the lecture. A half dozen of them would stand along each wall of the dining hall. Their job was to scan the audience and look for any staff members who might be falling asleep, looking disagreeable about anything being said, not paying attention, whatever. After the briefing or lecture, the guilty parties were hauled into the ethics section of their unit and worked over for "not being with the program." We've all heard similar stories, but usually they are associated with Red China or East Germany, not an officially recognized church in the United States of America.

The end result of these tactics was that David instilled such fear in people that if he gave an order and someone misinterpreted it and did something wrong, that person was certain they would be crushed. People became stimulus response robots. Fear pervaded the base, and, no doubt, there are people still there, as well as those who have left, who are scarred by the abuse.

I have mentioned the way David compensated for his small size at school by picking fights, but I am positive that there was another, much more important, influence that shaped the way he behaved as leader of the church. And this influence was L. Ron Hubbard himself.

Back in Mount Carmel, a lot of guys joined one of the branches of the military after high school. One weekend after boot camp, I was back home, hanging out, and there was a guy who had joined the Air Force and also was on leave. We were just sitting around talking, and I, as well as some others, noticed that this guy was now talking with a southern accent. Somewhere in the Air Force he had picked up a southern accent! People from Mount Carmel do not talk like that. We said nothing but figured that he was not being himself. It was like he was wearing the personality of someone else, probably a superior. Scientology calls this being in another person's valence. *Valence* is just a fancy word for identity.

I never met or worked with L. Ron Hubbard, but I have known a number of people who did—quite a few, in fact, including some of the original messengers who were with him on the *Apollo*. All have told me that he could be absolutely horrible to work with at times. Just a frothing, screaming madman when he was in a foul mood and things were not going well around him. David worked with him enough to witness these outbursts many, many times. Unlike everybody else who also saw these tantrums, David apparently used these as mentoring experiences. He, of course, adopted them with the energy and dedication that he did everything else in Scientology. He has taken LRH's valence, I am convinced of it.

But Hubbard also had a sunny side. He could be compassionate and caring, and his general demeanor was pretty cheerful. In fact, I am told that he was more often sunny than thundering. David must never have paid attention to that part of Hubbard's personality, because in my many last years of associating with David, the sun rarely, if ever, shone.

SIXTEEN

ASSESSING MY SON

Power tends to corrupt,
and absolute power corrupts absolutely.
Great men are almost always bad men.

—Lord Acton, British historian
and member of Parliament

THAT, IN A NUTSHELL, DESCRIBES WHAT HAPPENED TO DAVID Miscavige after he joined the Sea Org in 1976. The dynamics there were vastly different from what he grew up with at home. The Sea Org has a rigid hierarchy, and the higher one moves on the ladder, the more power one accumulates. David entered this environment right after leaving home, where he had me and his mother, as well as his siblings, kids at school and his teachers, who could exercise some restraint on him if he got out of line. In the Sea Org, the game was much like Chutes and Ladders, where you could climb high quickly but slide down just as quickly. He had entered a more dynamic situation and relished it. If you were energetic and gung-ho, you could climb the ladder rapidly.

By virtue of his status as a Commodore's Messenger, he had already been granted a considerable amount of leverage over most other Sea Org members, even those who had been in Scientology for decades. That first assignment of his, which I mentioned earlier, conferred great disciplinary powers on him when he was sent on a mission, and he used those powers liberally but not in a good way. A friend told me that David once watched her work on a cleaning detail. He stood there with arms folded for a few minutes and then disappeared. A short time later, her superior came around and began yelling at her for not working fast enough. On two other occasions, David returned, observed her work and complained to her superior; she got two more lectures about not working hard enough.

Later on, David became the person in charge of running all the missions, a promotion that increased his power. By virtue of that job, he could affect any organization in the entire Scientology network.

I've already described how David, at the expense of executives senior to him in the Commodore's Messenger Organization, made himself indispensable to L. Ron Hubbard while in his position as Special Pjt Ops. Part of this involved a corporate restructuring of the entire church that established three distinct entities that were, in theory, meant to serve as checks and balances on one another and thus stabilize Scientology for the future. The three organizations were the Church of Spiritual Technology (CST), which was the final repository for all of Hubbard's Scientology materials; the Religious Technology Center (RTC), which owns the trademarks and advanced materials of Scientology; and the Church of Scientology International (CSI), which manages the church and all related entities. Boards of trustees with lifetime appointments were established. When the church settled its long-running battle for tax exemption with the IRS in 1993, the documents filed with the IRS included the board appointments, so there is a record of the names. A good friend of mine, Terri Gamboa, was appointed a trustee of CST while she was in the Sea Org, but she never knew it until years after she had left the organization and saw the incorporation papers that are now public record. David, it seems, never told her of her appointment.

David ultimately became chairman of the board of RTC, though for several years he was occupied with another job. One reason for the corporate reorganization was to create legal separation between Hubbard and church operations. The solution was creation of an organization ostensibly designed to promote his literary affairs. This new unit was called Author Services, Inc. (ASI), and David was its head. He oversaw every aspect of ASI, including Hubbard's income and finances. Hubbard, though in seclusion, was still viewed as the head of all Scientology. All authority rested with him, and thus a system of checks and balances was unnecessary.

ASI's finance department invested Hubbard's money from time to time. A couple of employees made bad investments, and each lost $1 million of Hubbard's money. Both were removed. Dave and Pat Broeker then decided that they would take over the investments. Pat, as I mentioned before, was an old friend of David's from their days at the base in La Quinta. Pat and his wife, Annie, were Hubbard's closest aides during the last years of his life. Terri Gamboa, who also worked at ASI, says the two friends became heavily involved in speculation in oil wells using Hubbard's money.

A bit more about Terri: her mother, Yvonne Gillham, was considered royalty in Scientology; she was a dynamic, charismatic woman who headed Scientology's Celebrity Centre for years. Terri was one of Hubbard's messengers aboard the *Apollo* and as such held important executive positions in later years. When ASI was formed, Terri became its executive director, so she was in a position to know everything that went on, including the details of the investments that David and Pat Broeker were making. Terri claims that, through their financial wizardry, the two lost a ton of Hubbard's money in oil wells that turned up dry. Terri says the way David broke the news to the ASI staff was not "Pat and I lost the money." It was "We [meaning the whole organization, ASI] lost the money and now you [again meaning ASI] need to make it back."

She says that David became intent on recouping the losses before Hubbard found out. The plan he came up with included selling expensive special editions of Hubbard's books and art prints of book covers. Terri says that the staff of ASI was pushed hard to sell these items, and soon they were making $500,000 or more per week from these items alone.

David's brutal side began to appear more and more often. Once, he ordered every person at ASI to spit on a staff member who had fallen out of favor with David. According to that former staff member, the episode occurred while he was being interrogated on the E-meter with all ASI staffers watching while David shouted questions at him. To their credit, everyone but David and one other person refused to spit on the man; David and his accomplice chewed tobacco before their despicable display. The church has long denied that David engages in punishment of this kind.

For many years, David and Pat Broeker were close friends, confidants and confederates. After Hubbard's death, Pat and Annie were essentially the leaders of Scientology. Hubbard was said to have given them Sea Org ranks in a published issue before his death that basically cemented their authority over everyone else in the Sea Org. The authorship of that issue is open to dispute, however, and David had a different idea about who should control Scientology. A power struggle ensued between the erstwhile friends. A year later, David won.

Pat held one important pawn in the struggle: Scientology's most advanced technical materials in the form of Hubbard's own auditing folders, as well as notes that contained the instructions for higher levels of spiritual attainment that had yet to be released or even codified. That work was meant to fall to senior technical people after Hubbard's demise. Broeker had these materials securely locked away in a location where Dave could not get at them. This gave Pat leverage. According to Mark Fisher, David's former assistant who oversaw corporate liaisons between David and the different entities he was involved with, the only other person who knew the location of the unreleased technical materials was Annie, Broeker's wife, and Dave went to work on her. Eventually, he pried from Annie where the materials were hidden. Former Scientology executive Marty Rathbun told the *Tampa Bay Times* that he and David executed a plan to get the materials from Pat and Annie. According to Rathbun, David arranged a meeting with lawyers in Washington, D.C., that both he and Pat had to attend. Meanwhile, Rathbun positioned about 20 men outside the Broekers' ranch in Barstow, California. During a layover in Chicago, David called Rathbun and gave the signal to grab the materials. Rathbun says he then fed the caretaker at the Broekers' ranch a line that the FBI was going to raid the place in two hours. The story worked. Rathbun's men were let in and they carted the materials away, storing them safely at the Int base near Hemet. The church has consistently denied the accounts of former executives as the lies of disgruntled apostates.

His one and only chip now gone, Broeker, too, was soon gone. At that point, sometime in 1987, David gained uncontested power over Scientology. Now no one in all of Scientology had the authority or courage to tell him no. The fact of his struggle with the Broekers is the only proof I need that Hubbard never selected David to succeed him.

David left Los Angeles and moved back to the Int base. His first order of business was to clean house at the Religious Technology Center, purging the executives and staff there whom he believed had sided with Pat during the power struggle. In actual fact, they had simply been following Pat's directions while David was in Los Angeles running Author Services.

To revisit Lord Acton, "absolute power corrupts absolutely." I am not so arrogant as to presume that if I ever found myself in a position of holding absolute power that it wouldn't affect me in ways I cannot imagine, so I can only speculate about what may have contributed to David's corruption. And, for certain, he has become corrupt. When I compare the happy, fun-loving boy I raised to the man he has become, the images of Dr. Jekyll and Mr. Hyde spring immediately to mind.

In his position of absolute authority in Scientology, David became surrounded more and more by brownnosers and yes-men and -women. He never went anywhere without an entourage, so if a low-level executive thought that what David was proposing was nuts, objecting would have been political suicide. I suppose that after everyone agrees with your every pronouncement long enough, you begin to believe that you can do no wrong, and this certainly happened with Dave.

The more elevated he became in the eyes of his associates, however, the more he tended to express exasperation with them. The traits I mentioned earlier became more and more evident: the sharp rebukes became daily occurrences and the tongue-lashings more brutal. As time went on, David began to express his dislike for the base and its people. It got to the point that, during the week, when staff members dressed in uniforms, David and his closest associates dressed in civilian clothes. On weekends, when staffers dressed in civvies, David dressed in full Sea

Org uniform. The less he associated with people on the base the better, he felt, and this distinction in dress made the point symbolically.

None of these changes happened overnight. For years, he ate his meals in the dining room with the rest of the crew. He flew in coach or business class, not the private jets he takes today. His uniforms, while better tailored, essentially matched everyone else's. His office was of the same size and had the same furnishings as those of other RTC executives. The room that he and his wife lived in was nicer than other rooms, but he paid for the special features out of his own pocket.

One thing that anybody who has known him will affirm: David has the capacity to work very hard. It was nothing for him to work through the night if that was what the task at hand required, at least in the years before he assumed full control of the church. Basically, he could outwork anybody, and, to be honest, he was probably smarter than anybody around him. That is a great combination if it is driven by good intentions.

I recall one Saturday morning in the mid-1980s when he came up to Gold from Author Services in Los Angeles. He had been up all night working on reports that would be sent to Hubbard, and someone who was returning to the base drove David's van while he slept on the carpeted floor in the back. When the van arrived at the base, he was still sound asleep, and I carried him from the van to his room, just as I had done when he was a little kid.

Beyond the usual day-to-day concerns and headaches of the base demanding his work and attention, there was another factor pulling at David—the seductive lure of celebrity, most particularly in the person of Tom Cruise. This began around 1990, when Cruise was preparing to shoot *Days of Thunder*. Dave went to Daytona, Florida, where Tom was doing research for his role. When David returned to the base, he pulled his top executives into a conference room and showed them a video of Tom and him jumping out of an airplane and skydiving in tandem. The time they spent together obviously left David deeply impressed with the PR potential that Cruise could lend to Scientology. And to Dave.

The first time Tom came to the base, which also was their first meeting, David was on pins and needles, wanting to be sure that everything would be suitably impressive. At that time it was very hush-hush that Tom was even involved with Scientology. All the records of his auditing sessions were kept in folders labeled with his given name, Thomas Mapother. Tom had been audited in Los Angeles by auditors who were not in the Sea Org, and he was then married to Mimi Rogers, the daughter of Phil Spickler, a longtime and noted Scientologist. Spickler had run afoul of the organization some years before and had been excommunicated, so to speak. David desperately wanted to get matters under tighter control—that is, under *his* control—and one of his top lieutenants, Greg Wilhere, had finally arranged to bring Tom to the base for a stay and some auditing.

David orchestrated every detail for maximum impact on his guest. A special dinner was prepared by Hubbard's former chef to be served at the base swimming pool/recreational area, which had been given a complete makeover some years before (for just such occasions). Now the area looked like a clipper ship, complete with 50-foot masts with sails, a teak deck and even a lifeboat. Nothing had been overlooked. Schedules in Los Angeles did not cooperate, however, and Tom was late arriving. The appointed hour came and went, as did the next two hours. David paced around anxiously, demanding, "Are they here yet?"

Finally, four hours after his scheduled arrival, Tom appeared but told Greg that he just wanted to settle in and get to bed and that he and Dave could meet the next morning. When Greg delivered the news to

David, he hit the roof. However, things smoothed out the next day, and Dave and Tom hit it off.

Up on the hillside, behind a house that had been prepared for Hubbard to live in (but was never used), stood a crude rifle range. David had developed an interest in guns at one point, perhaps a delayed reaction from when I took him shooting when he was about eight. He and Tom used the range and had a great time. Several days before Tom's next visit, he made David a present of an automated skeet launcher to replace the manually operated one they had used on Tom's first trip. David immediately called for a complete renovation of the shooting range and had work crews up day and night for three days totally redoing it, including adding a bunker for the new skeet launcher. The purpose was solely to impress Tom Cruise.

I did not see them interact much, but I have been told that they developed a sort of brotherly competitive spirit, each trying to outdo the other. One time, they allegedly raced through Los Angeles in separate cars, running red lights, each trying to beat the other to their destination.

David's obsession with winning at all costs manifested in other ways too. He returned from a vacation to Pennsylvania one year and brought back the game Trivial Pursuit. It was all the rage at the time, but he found it nearly impossible because, while he was always bright, his general knowledge of geography, literature, the arts and so on was lacking because he never finished school. Other close associates of his were similarly ignorant, so when Dave played Trivial Pursuit, he always insisted that his team include a staff member who was up on popular culture and general knowledge to ensure that he always won.

Given all that, Dave's preoccupation with winning ties in with the analysis that follows. In 1953, Hubbard wrote an essay in which he detailed characteristics of a toxic personality type. He listed the following traits as indicative of such a personality (and here I am paraphrasing the original). Each point is followed by a father's analysis.

1. *If something unfortunate happens to a person, the toxic personality thinks that the misfortune is either ridiculous, a mere trifle, or that the person deserves it.*

I once contracted scabies from sleeping on an unclean mattress at Gold. Scabies is a contagious itch caused by a tiny mite that gets under the skin. It is horrible. The itching drives you nuts. I saw Dave while I was infected, and he shouted, "Don't get near me! Stay away from me!" He was afraid that I might infect him. He had no concern for me at all. It was all about him. The infection got so bad that I left the base and stayed with a Scientologist in LA, where I could lie out in the sun to help kill the mites.

2. *If someone does something to the toxic personality, the toxic person always regards what happened as extremely important and egregiously bad and thinks the damage can never be overcome.*

A common complaint of David's was how overloaded he was with work sent to him by staff from the various units on the base. His office building was called Building 50 (based on its designation on a property use plan), and it had a large open conference room on the ground floor. He regularly brought the musicians to that room and showed us the heavy cardboard boxes of submissions lined up around its perimeter. "Look at this," he would bark. "Look at the crap I get from you guys. I have to check everything because nobody on the entire base can be trusted. Look what you are doing to me!"

That was a standard refrain: how overworked he was because he was the only one who could be counted on to get things done.

If David ever felt that someone had crossed him, that person would go into his black book forever. You could never mitigate the damage to David if you got on his bad side. No amends would ever be acceptable. One example was Marc Yager, a onetime friend of David's who served for years as the head of the CMO and worked with David in RTC as Inspector General for Administration. Marc was the poor sap who spent that whole year living in the swamp at Gold after he crossed David, although no one ever learned exactly what had happened. Some years later, when I needed to make up for something David regarded as damaging to him, Marc told me (in exactly these words): "I don't know how you are ever going to make up the damage to COB."

Even those convicted of crimes in courts of law can pay their debt to society and go on with their lives. Not so with David. He will hold a grudge until the end of time.

3. *Anything that another person can do is without real value, according to the toxic personality, or can be done better by someone else.*

Because of my sales experience, I helped the salespeople in Los Angeles improve their skills at David's behest. I trained them by using simple Scientology principles such as having good communication, getting agreement bit by bit, and so on. Every person I trained wound up being able to sell.

Later, when I was no longer doing that training, sales began to flag in some areas. When Dave learned that the organizations were naming me as the person who had helped them, his comment was "Come on, man. I could fart more sales than you."

This speaks to perhaps the worst thing that anybody in an executive position can do. A good organization will always be stronger and more effective than a single individual, no matter how capable that individual is. A manager can wreck an organization by destabilizing the line of authority—by reaching down to lower echelons and bypassing those who are supposed to have authority over the area. I observed David for nearly 27 years in the Sea Org, and this was his stock-in-trade: jumping the chain of command.

He might be riding around the base on his motorcycle when he spotted one of the gardeners. He would go over and talk to her and verbally give her an order to do something that was completely off that day's to-do list. It might not even be her job, yet he would expect her to do it. Let's count the number of echelons jumped in this simple one-minute conversation: the gardener's direct supervisor, the head of the grounds department, the head of the Estates Division, that person's direct senior supervisor, the head of Golden Era Productions, the CMO unit assigned to oversee all of Gold and the executive in the next-higher CMO organization, which is called CMO International and tasked with overseeing Gold from an international perspective. One 30-minute tour of the base per day might find David issuing several of these random un-coordinated orders. The havoc that his chronic bypassing caused would be hard to describe and impossible to catalog, since most of it was not written down but issued only verbally.

4. *The toxic personality tends to be either sexually repressed or perverted.*

A basic Scientology concept is that life in its many forms is a matter of simply trying to survive. Scientology divides this urge to survive into eight separate dynamics, as Hubbard called them, that mirror the activities of life and the universe:

- Survival for oneself
- Survival through sex and the family
- Survival through groups
- Survival as part of humankind
- Survival as part of all living things—plants and animals
- Survival as part of the physical universe
- Survival as spirits or universal thought
- Survival through infinity, the Supreme Being, God, the Creator

Hubbard often talked about the second dynamic in his writings and lectures, noting how most people had hang-ups about sex, but he more or less dismissed these as trifling compared to the deeper issues that he felt posed much greater blocks to spiritual advancement. Hubbard mostly viewed relationship or marital blowups as distractions from the important work Scientology has to do to "clear the planet," Scientology's rallying cry to achieve its aims of a civilization free of crime, insanity and war. In the early days of the Sea Organization, Hubbard was loath to regulate Sea Org members' personal lives, but in the late 1970s, he finally approved an issue written by one of his messengers that put the kibosh on sexual relations among unmarried Sea Org members.

David got behind the new regulations, but over time he seemed to be dead set against the second dynamic in all its forms and manifestations. His attitude seemed to be that staff members, and by extension all people on planet Earth, were more concerned about sex and having kids than with helping him expand Scientology. He went to extremes to make his displeasure with "the 2D" felt.

The culture of the Sea Org with respect to sex and the family began to change. The group and its important work had always taken precedence over the family, but as David's influence as Scientology's new leader seeped down through the Sea Org hierarchy, the effects would be seen as shocking to the average person. What follows are a few examples of actions taken while he was at the helm.

Anyone in his org, RTC, who was married to someone working in a different unit on the base either had to divorce the spouse or leave RTC, to be posted to another unit. Some staff actually divorced their longtime spouses.

Husbands and wives often were split up when one was assigned to an outlying organization, sometimes for years at a time. One couple I know were separated for several years when the husband was sent to take an executive position in England while the wife remained at Gold. That was not the only instance, not by a long shot. With other restrictions, on travel and time off, for example, even people with a spouse working in Los Angeles might as well have been in Timbuktu given how infrequently they were able to see each other.

Women on the base were forbidden to have children, and I know that several former Sea Org members have claimed that they were pressured by colleagues or supervisors to have an abortion. I also know that if a couple wanted to keep a child, they were sent off the base to inferior postings. The church has denied that it has pressured anyone to have an abortion.

People who already had children when they came to the base were not allowed to live with their children. Instead, their kids were kept at another facility ten miles away. Some staff members who had children in Los Angeles were allowed to drive down on Saturdays to spend the day with them. "Family time," it was called. Parents at the Los Angeles organizations initially had one hour each day to spend with their children. Then, under some pretext, family time was canceled, which created a great deal of stress for many parents and their children. After that, parents and their children had limited opportunities to see each other. My granddaughter Jenna Miscavige Hill wrote in her book that she had seen her parents only a few times over the course of several years and even then only briefly.

In the last decade I lived at the base, marriages were exceedingly rare. Except for one, I am not aware of any marriages between staff members, a restriction that, I am told, has only recently been relaxed.

Any memos or issues that needed to be written to enforce these rules were written by others so as to put a layer of plausible deniability between their originator and enforcement of the decrees, but I am positive that any such orders came from David.

The final example I'll mention comes under the heading of perversion. I know that former Scientology executive Tom DeVocht and others have claimed that David has read out loud the sexual activities of individuals as confessed in their auditing sessions. Friends of mine have also observed this. Scientology representatives have denied it, saying that David has always "rigorously upheld the sanctity and confidentiality of ministerial communications."

5.   *The subject of food and eating is restricted by the toxic personality.*

While David's own food allowance runs into many hundreds of dollars each week, the food allowance for staff members at the base was sometimes reduced to less than a dollar per person per meal. That is less than $20 to feed someone for an entire week—while that person is working upward of 100 hours.

The galley staff performed miracles with such paltry allowances, and somehow people remained fed. The usual punishment in regard to food was to restrict an offending staff member to plain rice and beans for every meal until that person reformed. This could sometimes go on for weeks or months.

One time, Becky was assigned to a diet of rice and beans. We were at a meal, and I lifted a piece of meat from my plate and moved it toward hers. Another person sitting at our table said that if I did that, he would report me. As I said earlier, people become trapped by their own agreement to certain rules. This person was agreeing to the rules of the group, though left to his own devices, he would not have cared less what Becky ate. Why would he have reported me? One rule was that if you observed someone breaking the rules and did not report that person, you would be considered as guilty as the offender, for something as trivial as sharing food. I have never lived in East Germany or North Korea, but I am guessing similar regulations were being enforced there too.

David, meanwhile, was dining on New Zealand lamb or Maine lobster, with a personal chef on call for him, his wife and closest circle. Two entrees were prepared for each meal, in case one was not to his liking. One of the facilities on the base had a refrigerator that was about six feet wide and stocked with foods especially—and only—for David and his wife.

During my nearly 27 years in the Sea Org with my son David, I observed in him on numerous occasions each of the traits I have described. I wish I was not writing this, but it is the truth, and other people I know would say and have said the same.

A book by Harvard psychologist Martha Stout, *The Sociopath Next Door,* is based on her decades of study of toxic personalities. In it she claims that one in 25 people in the United States suffers from a mental disorder that leaves them without a conscience. Such people, she writes, never feel guilt, shame or remorse. She contends that, just as some babies are born without a hand or a limb, sociopaths are born without a conscience.

Further, she writes that few are the deranged killers we see in movies or read about in the news; rather, one of the chief characteristics of these conscienceless people is a charisma that can make them more interesting, more charming, more spontaneous, more intense and more appealing than other people. Not all people who have these traits are sociopaths, of course, but because of their ability to seduce others with their charm, they can be tricky to identify.

I will leave you to draw your own conclusions about why I mention Stout's book in this chapter. I have no doubt that it has been much harder for me to write this chapter than it is for you to read it. David, after all, is someone I have known since I peeked beneath that blanket outside the delivery room on April 30, 1960. He and I had countless wonderful moments together, and I loved him as I love all my children.

Yet the truth is the truth. I believe that people change throughout their lives but that those changes are not always for the better.

SEVENTEEN

ENOUGH IS ENOUGH

WHEN I REFLECT ON IT, THE WATERSHED MOMENT OC-
curred back on that August 1990 afternoon when the rain
poured down and mud slid off the mountain across State Route 79 and
onto base property. People busted their butts in their summer uniforms,
which were all white, mind you, to protect the property from water and
mudslide damage. By dinnertime, there was no one in Gold whose uniform was not soiled with mud.

Because Gold was responsible for the physical base itself, David
pinned the blame for the event squarely on the shoulders of every staff
member at Gold. And people bought it. Maybe some did not, and
maybe some thought that what he was raving about was crazy but realized it would be prudent to act on his demands.

From that day on, things never got better. Literally, never got better.
There might have been the rare good day but never a period of a week or
a month when staff could breathe a sigh of relief and think, We're okay
again. We're trusted. Never again were we in a position of trust. The

attitude expressed—and that attitude came straight from David and filtered down to Gold—is that we could not be counted on to initiate anything of worth or contribute to Scientology's purpose of making a better world. Imagine working in an environment such as that month after month, year after year.

So that you, the reader, understand, Scientology provides ways to deal with the situations that life throws at you. One of these tools is called the conditions formulas. A condition is simply a state of existence. Everything in the universe, including each of us, is in one condition or another. It might be good or it might be bad; that is beside the point. The theory behind the formulas that Hubbard developed is that one can take steps to change the condition one is in, whatever that may be, and improve it. If a person or a group determines what condition they are in, they can improve their lot by following the steps of the appropriate formula, and, sooner or later, things will improve. Except for Gold. We could not get an approval to move from one condition to the next higher one, no matter what we did or how long we worked at it. There was no forgiveness. It was like the sign over hell in Dante's *Divine Comedy:* "All hope abandon, ye who enter here."

As the years went by, that is how I began to feel. Without hope. We were never going to get out of that bad condition. When people are hopeless and held together as a group, people begin yelling and scream- ing at each other, and physical fights break out with people punched and thrown to the ground. Other people become apathetic and resigned: "Well, this is how I'm going to live for the rest of my days."

I could not give up hope and that was mainly due to Becky's im- ploring me, "It's going to get better. I know it." She is an incurable opti- mist and convinced me to stay. Maybe she's right, I thought. Maybe I'm taking everything too seriously.

It never got better.

Instead it got slightly worse, bit by bit, and year by year. If something is continually becoming slightly worse, it isn't going to start getting better unless you do something different. Either you have to change the way you are living or get out of there.

After the year 2000, regularly scheduled days off no longer existed. I did not have a day off for the next 12 years. Sea Org policy mandates that a person receive a day of liberty every two weeks. That became a dim memory at Gold. Each year every Sea Org member is supposed to have three weeks of leave. I could not get a leave to see my grandson get married. That was a real backbreaker for me. Then I could not get a leave to visit my brother when his wife died. That turned out to have been my last opportunity to see my brother alive. The next time I saw him, he was in a coffin. When my nephew called to tell me my brother had died, another Gold staff member was listening in on an extension in the same room. Everyone was subjected to these invasions of privacy, so you didn't even think about it. It was normal.

To attend my brother's funeral, I had to be accompanied by two "minders" plus an armed private investigator. The two minders were Greg Wilhere and Marion Pouw. My son Ronnie and his wife, Bitty, also were at the funeral, but Greg and Marion effectively prevented me from talking to them because they had left Scientology several years earlier. When that happened, I began thinking, Something really bad is going on here. Becky and I absolutely need to get out.

For many years we lived in apartments in Hemet about seven miles from the base. I told Becky, "We've got to get out of here and soon." Living quarters were being built at the compound itself behind the razor wire fences, and I felt that if we were going to leave, we would have to do it before staff moved into the on-base housing. We could have filled our car at the Hemet apartment and driven off. But Becky did not want to go. She still felt that things would improve. So we moved onto the base with the rest of Gold. This was in 2006. Razor wire, guards, and surveillance cameras—you may think that I am describing a prison. No, I am simply telling you what it was like while we were living at the international headquarters of the Church of Scientology.

As with everything else, the hypersecurity was gradually ramped up through the years. When the property was first purchased, the place was wide open; you could walk from one side of the property to the other at any point along the highway. As the facility became more developed, more security measures were added, again, a little at a time. A security force was put in place. Then fences. Then gates that were operated from the main guard booth. Then motion sensors on the fences. Then razor wire on top of the fences. Then cameras to watch cars along the highway. Then a lookout station halfway up the mountain in back of the property to keep watch. And it went on like that.

The housing on the base was well designed, functional and attractive. In fact, all the facilities on the base are top notch. The problem with perfection arises when living beings actually *use* the facilities. The beautiful homes you see profiled in *Architectural Digest* have been spit-shined for a photo shoot. David apparently thought that the housing on base should always be similarly pristine. So residents had to abide by various restrictions: you could not bring food or even coffee into your room, much less have your own little fridge or coffeemaker. You couldn't have televisions or DVD players. Each building had a commons room with a TV, but I never saw anybody watching it. People were too tired to do anything but to go to bed when they got home. If somebody did sit down to watch something on television, someone would have reported them for doing so when they should be sleeping. The TVs sat there idle, except maybe during Christmas or New Year's, when people had a few hours of free time.

A perfect living space was one that contained no personal items such as family photos, knick-knacks or a painting on the wall. The closets were built to hold only your uniforms and a few items of personal clothing. Each room had a bathroom, but unmarried people lived in dorms with six to a room, and I imagine things got pretty crowded in the mornings. In short, the living quarters were planned around the idea of the more sterile the better. But people had personal items nonetheless. Becky and I probably had more stuff than most, and we crammed it into every shelf space and corner.

A typical day at Gold went like this: breakfast in the dining hall was at 9:00 a.m., followed at 9:30 by the first of the day's roll calls. If you tried to grab a little extra sleep because you had been up late the night before, you would hustle down to breakfast, gulp it down and scurry out to muster. Breakfast was the same thing day in and day out: eggs, toast, granola, sometimes fruit. After eggs have been sitting in a serving pan for some time, they become cold. One day I walked into the galley and requested a couple of eggs hot off the griddle. I told the cook that I don't like cold eggs, and all the eggs on the line were cold. "Sorry," the cook replied, "it's against regulations." That's the level of control (and insanity) that permeated the place. Anything to make a person's life more miserable.

At morning muster, all hands were accounted for; security was supposed to find anybody who was missing. After listening to any important announcements, people hustled through the tunnel that ran underneath the highway and up to the course room for study time, which lasted until noon. During this time, people were supposed to be free to avail themselves of studies in Scientology. Mostly, though, people only studied materials designed to make them more productive in their jobs. The group and its needs always came first.

At noon, you hustled down to lunch. The meal was put out on serving carts, and you grabbed a plate, silverware and a glass, filled your plate and sat down at your table with about six or seven others. At the end of the meal, you cleaned off and stacked your dishes and then—hey, what do you know!—another muster at 12:30. More roll calls, more announcements and then it was off to work for the afternoon.

Dinner was at 5:00 p.m., followed by—what else?—another muster at 5:30. Then back to work until midnight, so long as we had no emergency to deal with or an upcoming event nightmare. At those times, any semblance of a schedule went out the window. Becky, who was working in marketing, would often be awakened in the middle of the night to go back in to the office and deal with something.

That was the schedule day after day. It was a pretty gray way to live for years on end.

By this time, 2006, we knew that at some point we would leave. For the next five or six years, we lived with the knowledge that someone would become aware of what Becky and I had talked about; if that happened, the chances of our ever leaving would have been exactly zero. As the father of COB, I would have had a guard on me around the clock all year long. The opportunities for someone to learn what we talked about were numerous because staff are given "security checks" for purposes of discovering any transgressions against the group, breaking of rules, and such. Secretly planning to leave certainly qualified. A security check is Scientology's version of an interrogation. Hubbard thought that an auditor using the E-meter would be effective in discovering whether a person was withholding knowledge of plots against him or the organization, and "sec checking" became a staple of church policy. After David took control of the church, security checks became more intense affairs with sometimes several people interrogating a suspect at the same time. When I look back on it, it reminds me of stories I heard of the Stasi in

East Germany. Needless to say, our conversations were never far from our thoughts, yet Becky and I managed to keep our plans to ourselves during all that time.

In late 2011, I called David and told him, "I've got to see you." He was not on the base at the time, but when he got back he arranged to see me. "Listen," I began, "you've got to get me out of the music department. I've been writing music every day, seven days a week, month after month, and none of it is getting approved. I am living a life of failure every day. I'll take a job waxing cars in the motorpool, or if you want to send me to Flag, I'll work there. But I can't live this way."

"I'll check it out," he promised.

Here is what had me in such desperate straits. I did my first paid job as a musician at age 13. I spent my time in the Marines studying music and playing in the Marine band. I played professionally for years, had a recording contract with Polydor Records and a writer's contract with Chappell Publishing. I ran the music department at Gold for many years.

Then a new person took over as music manager. Suddenly, anything I did became worthless, of no value, was not going to work and was deemed not suitable for any product. Each day I went to work, worked all day writing music, and each day it was, "Nah, it's dated," "It's trite," "It has no flavor," "You don't hold my attention at all," or (sarcastically) "Oh, I didn't know we were doing a period piece." Yet everything he did was wonderful. He even said to me once, "Your stuff doesn't stand up to mine in the least."

Imagine working at a job month after month and nothing you do is considered acceptable, whereas for years and years previously, almost everything was. You can understand why I pleaded with David to check it out.

He never checked it out.

Shortly thereafter I told Becky in no uncertain terms, "We're getting out of here."

"Okay, we'll do it."

We started planning our departure. One concern was how we could take all our stuff with us. We didn't want to leave valuable things behind. At the same time, we knew we were going to leave. A little background is in order here. On my birthday the previous year, Becky arranged for my daughters, Denise and Lori, to send me a bunch of little gifts. The idea was to present me with 75 gifts for my seventy-fifth birthday. Just before my birthday, five boxes of stuff arrived from Becky, Denise and Lori. All were small gifts, like a pen or a little voice recorder. The security guards obviously knew about this because all mail and packages were opened before being delivered. Talk about a violation of federal postal regulations, not to mention human rights!

This gave Becky an idea. Her mother's seventieth birthday was coming up, so she called her mom and told her that we were going to be sending her some stuff for her birthday. We were going to send her 70 "gifts." Unbelievably, Becky's plan worked. We mailed my mother-in-law my Scientology books and volumes of Hubbard's bulletins and policy letters. I did not want to leave those behind. They contained all the writings that I had found of such value for more than 40 years, and they meant a lot to me. The philosophy was one thing; life in the Sea Org was quite another. We mailed her a car-detailing kit. The security guards who checked every piece of outgoing mail never suspected what we were doing. We sent her a ton of stuff because we knew that we could not cram everything into our Ford Focus station wagon. That these security guards fell for our ruse does not speak highly of their intelligence. Becky's mom has never been involved with Scientology, yet we were sending her "gifts" of all of L. Ron Hubbard's bulletin and policy letter volumes about Scientology, more than 20 thick volumes. By the time her mother's birthday came and went, we still had not mailed everything we wanted, so we changed the story to "we are sending you Mother's Day gifts."

Because staff members were not allowed to have refrigerators, Becky and I would drive across the highway to the music studio, which had a refrigerator, every Sunday at 9:00 a.m. during the weekly period scheduled for cleaning and doing laundry. We would eat some cheese and salami or something. When we drove back to the housing complex area, I handed the guards some of my food, which they always appreciated. Feeding the watchdogs, you might say. It became a Sunday morning ritual as a way of getting them accustomed to what we were doing.

I had a couple of other things going for us as I worked out our plan. I was 76 years old. I was the father of the leader of the church. Nobody would suspect I was trying to escape at my age.

In an ironic turn of events, beginning in January 2012, David began showing up outside MCI around the time of Gold's evening musters. He'd wait until muster was over and then come visit with Becky and me for ten or fifteen minutes. We would shoot the breeze, laugh about stuff and reminisce about funny times. Sometimes he would grab us before muster, and we would be laughing about something while standing around the corner from the muster, and his secretary Laurisse would be trying to hush us so we wouldn't disturb the muster. It had been years since David had visited us like that. All the while, Becky and I knew we would soon be gone.

By late March 2012, I was getting nervous. "What if we get caught? What if the guard doesn't let us out the gate?" I'm not the nervous type, but, yeah, I was really nervous about what lay just ahead. We were going to leave the following Sunday morning, March 25. The day before, I gassed up the car in the motor pool. We had most everything packed up in our apartment. That night after work I began moving stuff out to the car. We had all our shoes in a mesh bag. As luck would have it, one of the security guards happened by on his motorcycle as I going out to the car.

"Hey, Sal, how ya doing?" I said, forcing a cheerful smile and hoping he wouldn't notice the beads of flop sweat that instantly appeared on my forehead.

"Hey, Ronnie. Going good," he replied. We shot the breeze for a bit before he rode off. That was a close call. He never connected the bag of shoes in my hands to anything suspicious. Sal, a close friend, could not in his wildest dreams imagine that I was loading personal effects into my car in preparation for an escape.

I went back inside, got a bag of clothes and came back out. Norman Starkey was going into the laundry room, which was right in front of my car. Norm was the trustee of L. Ron Hubbard's estate and one of the longest-serving and most legendary Sea Org members, since reduced by David's abuse to a shell of his formerly dynamic self.

"Hi, Ron. How's it going?"

"Good, man." I put the clothes in the car.

By the time I finished, the backseat was filled almost to the top. I had my horns in there. I had my Exer-Genies in there. (The Exer-Genie is an exercise device I have used for more than 50 years, the best little machine I have ever come across.) We jammed in everything we could.

The next morning we got up at seven. I took my cell phone and put it aside. Same with my pager. Because we were up so early, we had nearly two hours to pace around the room, check and recheck our list of everything we needed to have, and to worry. I had a little notebook with lists of everything we were going to take and what we were going to leave. Our car only held so much, so we had to decide what to sacrifice. I must have checked my list 50 times if I checked it once.

At 8:50 we took a deep breath, closed the door to our room behind us for (we hoped) the final time and walked out to the car. I started the engine, released the parking brake, put the car in reverse and backed out of my spot. Each moment, every action, was in sharp focus as if time had slowed to a standstill. I tried to look calm, but the butterfly effect was beating my insides to a pulp as we prepared to escape.

Only two security guards were on duty on Sunday mornings. One was in the main guard booth and the other in what was called the chase car, for dealing with people coming onto the property who should not be there as well as for chasing staff members who were attempting to escape. I drove slowly past the dining area and saw the chase car parked nearby, so we knew the guard was inside eating breakfast. The other guard was in the main booth. I drove up to the West Gate, which is 200 yards west of the main booth. Here goes nothing, I thought. If he calls me up to the booth, we're sunk. Jesus Christ, what if he doesn't open the gate? He's got to open the gate. Briefly, the rest of my life flashed before my eyes. I firmly believe that, had we been caught, Becky and I would have been locked up in a remote part of the base under 24-hour guard, and I would have spent the rest of my life like that. I never would have gotten out. Never.

My finger was shaking as I pressed the intercom buzzer to let him think I was going across the highway to the music studio, just as we did every Sunday morning at that time. He didn't even answer, just opened the gate. I inched the car through and out onto the road.

"Becky, we're turning left!"

I punched the gas and we peeled off down the highway, away from the base. I knew the guard would call me on my cell phone, which I had conveniently left in our room. "Hey, Ron, what are you doing? What's up? Hey, Ron! Answer me!" Then he would call the chase car guard from breakfast and say, "Hey, get up here to the booth, pronto!"

Meanwhile, I was hauling ass down the road. I knew that by the time the chase car got to the booth, I would be at an intersection a mile from the base, which meant I could take any of three routes. Turning right would take me to Interstate 10. Going straight led to U.S. Route 60 toward Los Angeles. Turning left would take us toward town. I turned left, figuring that the chase car would think I was headed for a major highway.

I turned right at the first stoplight, which put us out in the boondocks. We followed that road until we came to Interstate 215.

We had made it. We were *free*.

EIGHTEEN

BACK IN THE REAL WORLD

WE DROVE CROSS-COUNTRY FOR TWO AND A HALF DAYS until we reached Wisconsin, where Becky's family lived. It was a wonderful, liberating time. I was exhilarated. "Holy smokes, I'm free!" Becky was equally flipped out. We could do whatever we wanted. We could stop anywhere we wanted to eat, and we could eat whatever we felt like having. All those chains that I had allowed Scientology to put on me—and that I agreed were going to hold me down—were g-o-n-e! It was a wonderful feeling. It was like being able to breathe again after being suffocated.

It is hard to explain how it feels after more than 26 years of being nullified, told that you and your group are the worst group in the history of Scientology—and that L. Ron Hubbard had said so in memo after memo since Gold's formation—and that nothing you did could ever be right the first time. Yes, there were some good times mixed in—don't think I'm saying that it was all negative—but the bad times far outweighed the good.

While I lived at Gold, I had a case of eczema so bad that at times my sheets would be bloody from my violently scratching my legs. It would drive me nuts. I went to a doctor, who asked me if I had been under any stress. "No," I answered in all honesty. I was so used to the way things were that I sincerely did not believe I had stress in my life. Three months after we left, the eczema went away and never returned.

If you have built a prison for yourself little by little, brick by brick, and you are living in it, you don't know that you're in prison. By agreeing to restrictions and insanities, you are putting up your own barriers. You are building the walls. You are putting the bars in the window. That is how it happened, and that is how I ended up staying there for nearly 27 years.

It is probably how many groups in history have found themselves trapped. People can become trapped by their own thoughts. Let's face it: oppressors are always far fewer in number than the oppressed. Why don't the oppressed simply chop them up with hatchets or just stop listening to them? Because the oppressed have been told by the "authorities" that this is the way it has to be, so they believe it and they begin slowly putting up these barriers in their own minds. Next thing they know, they are living in this shell of a prison. That is the way it happens. There's no other way it can be done. I'm sure of it.

That was the prison I built for myself, and the authority at first was L. Ron Hubbard. Then David Miscavige, his unappointed successor, usurped the authority. David's approach, of keeping people thinking they were incapable and that he had to do everything (his constant refrain), caused people to feel sorry for him since he "had to do everything," and they listened to him because he was the authority figure. All these restrictions—you have to have your mail checked, you cannot go on liberty, you can't go to a store, and many more—each is another little bar for your jail cell. You build your own prison and you live in it.

It is fair to ask, why don't people simply leave? Here are some of the reasons: many people at Gold and other Sea Org installations have been in Scientology for 20, 30, 40 years or even longer, and they have zero savings. They live from week to week on their $50 allowance. They don't have a car. They have next to no Social Security. They have no particular skills that will get them a job in the outside world, and many have no place to go. Perhaps their parents have died, or they don't have sisters or brothers. If they left, they would literally be out on the street.

You hear stories about someone who has been in prison for 15 or 20 years, and after a while that's all he knows. He hangs out in the yard, he gets three meals a day, he has a place to sleep, he can watch TV. So eventually he is released, and what does he do? He commits another crime so he can go "home" again.

For the people at the base, these considerations are huge barriers to obtaining their freedom. People become willing to tolerate anything. How do they do it? I'll tell you how—they go numb. Their attitude becomes "I don't care what happens to me." That's how you can tolerate it. I adopted that attitude myself at times. We would be at one of the Saturday night briefings, and Gold would be getting ripped apart with Religious Technology Center staffers standing along the walls and spotting people in the audience who looked sour. I would sit comfortably in my chair thinking, I don't care what happens. That is a terrible state of mind, just terrible, believe me.

Those are just some factors that I think explain how intelligent, well-meaning, good-hearted people become involved in Scientology and stay in it long after their good sense screams at them to get out. These, however, are negative aspects. I think Scientology also has positive facets that keep people coming back for more.

Hubbard possessed an impressive vocabulary. He was a charismatic speaker, spicing his lectures with entertaining stories and humor, and he came across as an intelligent, well-meaning person. He could lecture for 90 minutes with no notes, simply speaking off the cuff. Whether he used his gifts to con people is not the issue here; taken at face value, he was impressive. He came off as learned. These characteristics carry some authority with people. And his public persona was jovial and easy to like. Listen to one of his recorded lectures and you can get a sense of what he was like at his best. Several lectures that he had filmed show him at his most engaging.

More important, his lectures contained principles and concepts that people found useful in their lives, regardless of whether he developed them himself or repackaged what others before him had said. He presented a perspective from which people could understand the factors in their lives more clearly, and he gave them concrete ways to apply his ideas.

After listening to a few more lectures or reading more of Hubbard's writings, a person would begin to develop some confidence in what he was saying. A and B worked, so the person begins to feel that C will also work. At some point along the line, the person continues to believe whatever he said. When faced with a new concept that they may not grasp immediately, this person thinks, Well, he's been right before; I guess he's right here too.

Later on, when this person's experience with more advanced teachings does not deliver the same insights as earlier, or when friction inevitably occurs because of the imperfect workings of the organization, the person resolves the cognitive dissonance that ensues by recalling the experiences that *were* positive and the principles that *did* work. I doubt a single person who has ever been involved with Scientology has not been rubbed the wrong way by the organization. I had my fair share in the nearly 27 years I was in it.

Probably the most degrading thing that happened to me in my whole career in the Sea Org was being "thrown overboard." This was a disgusting remnant of the days aboard the *Apollo* when Hubbard, in fits of pique, ordered that offending trainees and others be tossed over the side of the ship into the water while the ship's chaplain uttered some stupid incantation about committing one's sins to the deep and hoping that the victim would become a better person. Two crew members would grab the unlucky ones and literally toss them into the water 20 or more feet below. Thankfully, no one ever died as a result, but that is an example of the ruthlessness that Hubbard was capable of.

That little practice was resurrected at Gold during David's tenure. For some offense—the reason escapes me now—I was ordered to be "overboarded" once. At Gold this was done by marching the person out to the small lake that once was part of the golf course. A stone bridge had been built out to an island in the lake. I stood on the bridge, was allowed to take off only my shoes and wristwatch, the port captain recited the same stupid litany, and I was pushed off the bridge fully clothed into the murky water below. It was a ridiculous but degrading moment and accomplished nothing of any value, except to alienate me even further.

One of the others condemned to the same humiliation was an extremely overweight fellow. I thought to myself, This guy could actually drown. They pushed him off, and down he went. He disappeared below the surface and bobbed up gasping. I was actually relieved to know he would be all right physically, if not psychically.

Being overboarded was extreme, I'll admit. Most of the daily irritations were more minor but happened every day. I used to eat raw garlic or raw onions because they are good for my health. One day I went into the galley and asked a cook for an onion. She gave me one and off I went. At dinner that evening, I was sitting at my table when another cook came out and began lambasting me in front of everybody because I had taken the galley's *last* onion. I hadn't taken the last diamond from the crown jewels or the *Mona Lisa* from the Louvre; another cook had simply given me the last onion from the galley stores! This apparently reflected the stress this cook was under because of having a food budget of only three dollars per person per day, or one buck per meal. Being out of onions apparently stressed this cook to the point that someone needed to hear about it, and that person was me.

Such tension permeated every part of the organization. It was an ever-present part of life at Gold and a super effective way to build callouses on your social interactions. People were under extreme pressure to perform on their jobs, and the lack of adequate resources was never an acceptable excuse. Who knows? Maybe onion soup was on the menu for the next day, but with the last onion now gone, the cooks' menu planning was ruined.

Throughout our cross-country trip, Becky and I talked and talked and talked. We vented all the things we dared not voice while at the base or that we were too tired to say once we got home at night. Those few days were therapeutic. When we stopped for gas, we paid cash. When we stopped for food, we paid cash. When we booked a motel at night, we paid cash. The church is good at tracing credit card payments and therefore your route. So everything was strictly cash.

When we got to Iowa, Becky called her brother. He was visiting friends when she called, and she could overhear him saying to someone in the background, "Somebody get me a drink! I'm celebrating! Becky's coming home."

We went to Becky's mother's place in Whitewater, Wisconsin. I figured that was the only safe place we could go. Both of my daughters, Denise and Lori, are Scientologists, and if we had gone to them, the Scientology goons could have found us, and neither of my daughters would have prevented David's stooges from talking to us. Becky's mother is not a Scientologist, so they wouldn't dare barge into her place.

We settled in with her mother, who was happy to have us. We spent a while just enjoying our freedom. I must have gained 15 pounds. I could eat cherry pie any time I wanted to. Back on the base there was a kitchen in the music studio, but if you went in there at any time other than scheduled mealtimes, you would be in trouble if anyone saw you. Even for a drink of water. "What are you doing in here, Ron?" the music manager would say. I guess he thought that David Miscavige was the model executive, so he mimicked David's behavior.

Two weeks after we arrived, I was standing in the kitchen and saw our old friend Marion Pouw walk past the window, snooping. I went outside, and standing there were Marion and Greg Wilhere. As I have mentioned, these are two of David's top henchmen and they had finally tracked us down.

"Hey," they said cheerily, "I bet you're wondering why we didn't come here sooner." To them nothing had changed. They acted as if it was just like old times. "Wow, we thought you were going to go to Lori's place. You sure surprised us. Ha ha." They were laying it on real thick, pretending cheerfulness. "We thought you were going to go to Florida. That's why we weren't here sooner. Ha ha ha."

I was guarded but somewhat friendly. The conversation quickly turned to our returning to the base.

"I'm not going back. Come on, Greg," I said, "I escaped."

"You didn't escape. You blew!" he shot back, and he pulled out a Hubbard policy directive called "Leaving and Leaves," which describes the protocol to be followed when someone leaves staff. Of course, that policy is never applied when someone asks to leave. It is dragged out only when people from the base are trying to convince someone who has escaped, or blown, as they say, to return.

"Go to hell, man. I'm not reading that. I'm not going to keep living under that goddamn suppression." I was no longer surrounded by 400 people who were going to jump me if I talked that way. It was only two against one, and I would take those odds any day.

"Listen, guys, it's not okay that you came here, and I'm not going back," I told them.

"Okay, let's talk," they countered. I agreed.

The next day I met them in town in a parking lot.

"David wants to talk to you. Give me your cell phone number," Greg opened.

"Screw you, Greg. I'm not giving you my number. I'm through. You no longer have me!" By this time I was totally willing to use force on him.

"Okay," he said, "I have a message from Dave for you: 'Please, please come back! You don't have any idea what you're doing to me. Please come back.'" Greg was playing the part of a whiny Chihuahua to the hilt. One of them also told me that the security guard had to tell David that we had escaped, and the guard literally had to struggle to get the words out of his mouth. David's response to bad news is simply to shoot the messenger. The guard finally told him we had left, and David's response was, "In my wildest dreams this is something I never thought I would see." Well, in *my* wildest dreams I never thought I could end up living that way. As a prisoner. A virtual prisoner!

Greg saw that I still needed convincing. "Look," he argued, "if you come back, you can go to Flag. You can have your own apartment. There's cooking facilities. You can work whatever hours you want. And maybe, if you want, you can teach these young kids to sell. And you can play with the musicians if you want. And then, if you don't like that, you can do what you just did and leave again."

"Greg, I am not going back." I don't doubt for a second that the message he delivered came from Dave because of the words, "You don't have any idea what you're doing to me." What *I* was doing to *him?* Only one person in the world would have the balls to say that: my son David.

"Let us take you out to dinner. There's a real nice place we found and after we can go to a movie."

These schmucks actually had the nerve to think they were going to schmooze me into going back with dinner and a movie. They must have thought we were dating.

What the hell was this? These people were from outer space. They think that they can come to somebody who had to escape to get away from that life and that the person is now going to say, "Gee, guys, I'm sorry. Of course I'll come back." How much more wrong could they have been about a person like me? They seriously miscalculated if they thought they could flatter me into going back or that I would act contrite and say, "Aw, shucks, I'm sorry, guys. All right, we'll come back. We'll face the music."

That was the end of it. They were staying in a motel on the other side of town and getting around in a rented Jeep. They called every day. I never answered their calls. They must have called for a month.

Meanwhile, Denise and Lori and I had been talking frequently. It was like old times with them. They were glad to be back in touch and so was I. Denise even offered us the use of her husband's boat, a yacht that was moored at a marina in Clearwater. She said we'd be safe there. Denise had also been talking to Ronnie and had given him my phone number. I had no idea where Ronnie was living and no way of contacting him because he had left Scientology years before, in 2000. One day he called me out of the blue. It was a pleasant surprise.

"Ronnie! How are you doing? How did you get my number?"

"You buy vitamins from VitaCost, right? Well, they sent me one of your invoices thinking I was you, and it had your number on it."

I did not know at the time that Denise had given him my number. Both of us are named Ronald Miscavige. Ronnie buys supplements from VitaCost as well. Of course, it is completely illogical that they would send the invoice of someone living in California (where I had been ordering before we escaped) to someone living in Virginia, even with the same name, but I was so happy to speak to Ronnie that the point slipped past me. The VitaCost tale was what we called a shore story in the Sea Org, in other words, a lie. When I was talking to Denise later, I said, "Guess what? Ronnie called me!"

"Oh, really," she said, pretending she didn't know anything about it. "Wow, that's great, Dad. Now Ronnie's is a place where you should go. I'm sure he'll take care of you. He built a house. It has a guest room in case you ever came by." She talked me into going to Ronnie's house in Virginia.

The next time Ronnie called, he invited us to come down for a visit. A little while later, Becky and I flew down, and we stayed with Ronnie and his wife, Bitty, for a week and had a great time.

When we got back to Whitewater, I called the motel where Greg and Marion were staying. I asked to speak with Greg Wilhere and was told that they had checked out the day after Becky and I flew down to Virginia. The church has ways of tracking people when they fly, and that is how they knew we had gone to Virginia. They had stayed in Wisconsin for a month after I had told them we would never go back and even though I never took a single one of their calls. Why did they stay? Simple: they did not want to return and tell COB, "We couldn't get them back." You can be sure they were both in a world of hurt after they limped back onto the base.

That August, Becky and I drove down to Virginia, stopping in Indiana to visit Becky's dad and my old hometown of Mount Carmel on the way. We stayed with Ronnie for nearly a year. Becky got a job, and

I sold Exer-Genies and began looking around for gigs as a musician. I also started reading the Internet and began finding out stuff about L. Ron Hubbard that I had never known, such as his war record, his previous marriages and so on. I got in touch with other people I knew from the base who also had left. One was Hubbard's granddaughter Roanne Horwich, who left after I did. When we spoke, she said she had been planning to blow that same Sunday as well but couldn't because we got out first. She felt she had to make sure there was not some general concern with people escaping, so she waited a month before driving out the gate.

I began contacting other people from the base who had left: Marc Headley, Steve Hall, Joe Caneen and a really good friend, Fernando Gamboa, the longtime drummer for the Gold musicians. As I talked to them and read more on the Internet, I began to see how I had been duped. L. Ron Hubbard was not the heavenly soul the church made him out to be. Not even close. Despite his many obvious warts, however, he did codify a lot of things that he learned from other people and advanced their theories with discoveries of his own. That may be hard to fathom for anyone who has read news stories about Scientology and Hubbard. I don't doubt that Hubbard read and learned from Aleister Crowley, the British occultist and writer, or that he and Jack Parsons were dabbling in black magic and planning to create a moonchild (a perfect soul, captured through black magic rituals). I don't doubt that Hubbard was a con man. But I believe that each of us is capable of engaging in negative or positive behavior. Whichever you choose is your decision as an individual. Your experiential track will lead you to adopt certain moral codes or develop a conscience, or whatever you want to call it, and that will deter you from acting out certain behaviors. A person can choose to live a fruitful, productive life helping people, and I firmly believe that you get the most benefit out of life that way. If you begin doing evil stuff, it is going to come back to you somehow.

If there is one point where I think Scientology falls down it is this: Hubbard stated time and time again that Scientology was a scientific approach to the mind and life. He wrote that Scientology was the meeting ground between science and religion. The very large problem with that is that science progresses in a precise way. Someone advances a theory and tests it out. Other scientists replicate the experiments that validate or invalidate the original theory. Others weigh in on the subject. Other ideas are tossed around, some good, some not so good. Advances come from that process. That's science. When someone asserts, "This is the way it is, period," that is not science. That is authoritarianism and it quickly becomes a cult, which is what Scientology is today.

Ever since Hubbard's death in 1986, Scientology has stopped progressing and even fossilized. That isn't science, if indeed it ever was.

At any rate, down in Virginia, Becky and I got along great with Ronnie and Bitty, and life was good. But Ronnie's daughter, Jenna, and grandkids were out in San Diego. Bitty had been spending a lot of time there, and, I wondered, what if he decides to move out there with them? He was going out to visit all the time, so I finally told Ronnie that we were going to move back to Wisconsin. We had been in Virginia for nearly a year, but it was time to settle down near Becky's mother and her relatives, a situation that would be more supportive than our going it alone in Virginia. I like the weather in Wisconsin better—I like the seasons and the cold up there. Having grown up in Pennsylvania, I came to enjoy it.

Becky got a job with the same chain as an assistant store manager in Wisconsin. In June 2013, we moved back in with her mother and began looking for a house. And that deserves a chapter of its own.

NINETEEN

A FINAL GESTURE

BEING THE FATHER OF THE LEADER OF SCIENTOLOGY IS A
sword that cuts both ways. I've already written about some of the
advantages that came with that relationship. On my birthday, Dave
would send me a really nice meal from a good LA restaurant, a full meal
like an Italian dinner, with a basket of salamis to accompany the spread,
and Becky and I could enjoy the dinner as long as we wanted that evening. We were excused from the evening muster. He never called, but
he always sent a nice meal. Some of the crew were jealous of the gesture,
and I could sense it as they scurried out of the dining room to roll call.

Also, that personal communication channel was open most of the
time if I needed or wanted it. Sometimes we would run into each other
when he was on the base and just chat for 15 minutes or so.

For my seventieth birthday, Tom Cruise sent me an enormous
blown-glass vase, literally the size of an aquarium (in fact, it was later
used as such), and it was full of flowers. Along with that he sent me a
very nice Harman/Kardon sound system that I still use. One Christmas,

John Travolta sent me DVDs of all his movies. Another time, Tom gave me a coffee table book on jazz that must have weighed 20 pounds.

Whatever perks I gained from my relationship with David came at a price, however. The security guards, for example, went out of their way to prove that I was not going to receive any special treatment. On Sunday mornings, we had cleaning time, and that afternoon security guards inspected everybody's rooms. They complained that Becky and I had the worst-looking room they had ever inspected. Why? Because we had a bunch of family photos on the shelves. I had been in other people's rooms and the guards' assertion was simply not true. One security guard actually said that he was repulsed when he went into our room. We were made to go look at his room, and there was not a single personal item anywhere. Not one photo, not a single book, nothing. Just bare furniture. That was supposed to be a model room, neat as a pin. All it proved to me is that he did not own anything.

If I parked my car next to the motor pool in a space where the mechanics wanted to put a car, the reaction I got was, "What the #!@& are you doing? Get your car the %!#!* out of here!" If someone else did the same thing it was, "Tsk, tsk, that's a no-no."

I think that people sometimes went out of their way to show me that they were not intimidated because I was COB's father—they were going to let me have it. The truth probably is that they were taking out on me what they wished they could do to COB.

I left all that behind when we escaped in March 2012. Some time later, during the time we were in Virginia, I decided to write Dave a letter. I wanted to let him know why we escaped. "If you are wondering why I left," I began and proceeded to explain the different issues that had led up to my decision: working every day week after week, month after month, without getting anything approved; literally begging him to get me another job so I could produce something of value; not being able to make phone calls without someone listening in; having my mail opened; not being able to go to a store; not having a day off; and so on. That letter was sent back by Marion Pouw, and I was told that David had not seen it because it was "antagonistic."

Later, I wrote another letter saying that because of my years in the Sea Org, I had not been paying much into Social Security and that I would like some financial help. This time he answered and sent me $100,000 so I could buy a house.

Loretta had died in 2005 from chronic obstructive pulmonary disease. She had been on life support for some time, and my daughters finally made the decision to take her off. From a Scientologist's perspective, Loretta—the being, the individual, the spirit—was either ready to leave her body or had already left, and only a physical shell was being kept alive. For what? It was time to allow her to move on. Her estate was divided among our children, and Dave gave me his share of the inheritance.

It is fair to ask how I reconcile this act of generosity with behaviors that most definitely qualify as selfish and corrupt to the core—the harm that Sea Org members, public Scientologists, the international Scientology network, the subjects of Dianetics and Scientology, as well as the legacy of L. Ron Hubbard himself have suffered under David's abusive leadership—these things are all well documented in a growing public record of news reports, documentaries and the accounts of former Scientologists. I wonder what in my letter reached him as he sat alone in his office, perhaps reading it in a quiet moment. I can't say for certain that it was the father-son bond we formed as he was growing up—the comical things we did together, the bench presses I made him do in the garage on winter evenings to stave off another asthma attack, our shared suffering as fans of the Eagles and Phillies. Maybe there still existed in him a tiny flame of humanity, of compassion. Or, to take a harder look, maybe the check was a public relations move, an investment to shut me up and make me go away, to hedge his bets against the possibility of a tabloid headline. I'd like to believe it was a spark of humanity, but after living under his leadership for almost 27 years in the Sea Org, I have doubts.

Regardless, we used that money to buy a house. Becky had gotten a good job in Milwaukee, but living in Whitewater meant nearly an hour's commute each way. We wanted to be closer to her work, so we looked for houses in West Allis, a Milwaukee suburb. We found a place that was perfect for us, cozy with a nice yard and a basement that I could use for my music. We bought the place in August 2013, and that was when the fun began and why I am telling my story.

TWENTY

"IF HE DIES, HE DIES. DON'T INTERVENE."

WE MADE PLANS TO MOVE INTO OUR NEW HOUSE. BECKY would have nearly two more hours in her day. I would continue selling Exer-Genies, but initially I would spend much of my time scouring secondhand shops and garage sales for everything we needed. After more than a year of living with Becky's mom and Ronnie, we were looking forward to settling down in a place of our own.

There were some other houses for sale in the neighborhood; one was in sight of ours, in fact. One day a neighbor spotted a man walking back and forth in the area while talking on his cell phone. She watched him for a while as he paced up and down the street. One thing I like about Wisconsin is that people here look out for each other. She grew suspicious, then picked up her phone and reported a prowler. Soon afterward, an officer in a patrol car saw a man peering through the glass in the door of a house for sale.

The officer approached the man and asked him what he was doing; he replied that he was just looking at houses. He refused to identify himself, which didn't sit too well with the officer. One thing led to another, and the officer, now joined by a detective who had also responded to the neighbor's call, arrested the man. They searched his car, which had been left with its motor running around the corner and alongside our new house. Now I ask you: Who leaves his motor running and walks around the corner to go snooping? Inside his car the officers found, among other things, a fake driver's license, seven license plates from five different states, a GPS tracking device, portable cell phone blockers, laptops, cameras, a stun gun, several handguns and rifles, ammunition, and, oh yes, a 30-inch-long homemade silencer.

Down at the station house, the man identified himself as Dwayne Powell, a private investigator from Florida. He said he had been following me for a year and a half and that his son Daniel had been working with him for the past year. David's gift of $100,000 so I could buy a house looks kind of cheap in light of the fact the church paid these two clowns way more than $500,000 to spy on me for more than a year and on an ongoing basis report back anything and everything I did between 8:00 a.m. and 8:00 p.m. To me, it is impossible to conclude that anyone besides David was behind the entire affair.

Dwayne was snooping around the house that day because of its location—our house was within sight. If Dwayne bought it, apparently being able to spy on me from an upstairs window would make his job a lot easier. He told the police that his job and his son's was to dig up dirt on me.

Meanwhile, Daniel Powell was unaware of his father's encounter with the police, but he finally learned that Dwayne had been arrested and went to the station, where Daniel, too, spoke to the police. Father and son independently said that they had been hired by the Church of

Scientology through another private investigation firm and that their main client was David Miscavige. Dwayne said that an intermediary was paying them $10,000 a week on behalf of the church.

Asked what he considered his and Dwayne's job to be, Daniel said, "We dig up dirt on this guy to make sure he can't do anything to hurt the church." As Daniel told it, the Powells wrote reports every day about what they had done; they sent these reports to "the client," who documented the reports. The PIs did not know what happened to the information after that.

They were especially on the lookout for anything I might say that denigrated David. David evidently did not want "the target," as they referred to me, talking to other people who had left the church and who might be saying bad things about him or the church. Furthermore, Daniel told the police that the church has a network of people out in the field (imagine a spider web with David at the center)—former Scientologists who are used to defuse any plan I or someone else might have. He explained that if, for example, he and his father learned that I was talking to someone else who had escaped from the church and might pose a threat, they would report it to the client, who would then relay the information to the PIs keeping an eye on the person I was talking to. Then, as Daniel understood it, an undercover agent for the church would go to work to defuse the situation. In other words, if I was planning to write a book and they found out about it, a supposed friend would call me and say, "Oh, Ron, you don't want to get into that. You want to retire," in an attempt to influence me to drop the idea. As it so happened, a so-called friend once used almost exactly those words when I was considering writing a book some years ago. According to the police report, Dwayne corroborated this, saying, "If Ron was doing anything that was deemed to be not in the best interests of the church, I would report to my contact, and the church would send people from LA to intervene and speak with Ron to correct his behaviors."

Daniel said that someone had relayed to them a message from David: that he just wanted his father to live his life and go off and retire in some out-of-the-way place. He and Dwayne were told that David was the leader of the Church of Scientology. That's true. I am his father. Also true. But the message also included this: I was the musical director of the church, and my music had become outdated, so David said to me one day, "Don't worry about it. Just go off and live your life," which, according to the Powells, I supposedly took to mean, "You're fired. Get the hell out of here. We don't want anything to do with you anymore. Leave." They also were told that I was writing books, one of which was entitled *My Son David*. Daniel also was told that Dave had paid me to not finish that book, which was how I got the money to buy our house. He also was told that David bought me a $5,000 trumpet to guarantee my silence. All complete nonsense, except, ironically, the part about writing a book—this book!

During the year and a half they followed me, Dwayne and Daniel told police, they sat behind me in restaurants to overhear my conversations. They snuck past me when I was using computers at the Whitewater library and peeked over my shoulder to take screenshots that showed whom I was emailing. They followed me wherever I drove. They put a GPS on my car. They pulled up next to me in parking lots and listened to my telephone conversations. They photographed me wherever I went. They went into stores and asked clerks what I had talked about. They followed Becky and me from Whitewater to Virginia, when we went to stay with Ronnie, and watched me there.

They even rifled through my trash. Each morning I make a "to-do" list for the day. The next day I tear it up and throw it in the garbage. The Powells had taped at least one of these lists back together and taken a photo of it. Detective Nick Pye of the West Allis Police Department saw the photo. The Powells also had photos of my computer screen from when I sat at the library emailing people. These are big-time invasions of privacy, arranged by the church for the express purpose of snooping into my life as deeply as they could. What other church does stuff like this?

Dwayne and Daniel Powell watched me come and go for more than a year. And they saw me reach for my cell phone that day in the parking lot at Aldi's.

Daniel saw me hunched over and grabbing my cell phone, and he told his father, "He looks like he's having heart problems." Dwayne relayed that information to his contact at the firm that hired him. Within minutes, David called Dwayne. This had never happened before. David's instructions still impact me: that if it was my time to die, Dwayne should let me die and not to intervene in any way.

Dwayne then said to Daniel, "I don't care what David says, if you see the old man on the ground, and he starts grabbing his chest, you call 911. But don't go help because if they get pictures of us helping, we can get sued because our client told us not to do anything."

That was the only time either of them talked to David and very likely the last. Dwayne told the police that he thought it was weird because, to his knowledge, none of the PIs had ever talked to David. Still, both Powells were concerned that if they lost this job, they would lose their cars, their homes and everything they had bought since they had been following me. If they'd had any common sense, they would have figured out that when you are riding the gravy train, as they had been for more than a year, the smart thing to do is pay all your bills and don't tie yourself down with a bunch of financial commitments because you never know how long the ride will last. Daniel told the police he had a monster truck, several Camaros, a Corvette and two motorcycles, as well as a bunch of guns, and that he and his dad each had a house. They were worried that if they lost the gig, they would lose it all. I don't know for sure, but I imagine they did and they have.

The butterfly effect is an interesting theory. If Dwayne had not let more than a year's worth of weekly $10,000 paychecks go to his head, maybe he would have been more cooperative when the officer asked him why he was prowling around the house that day. Who knows? They might still be cashing those fat checks even now. For certain, though, you would not be reading this book because I might never have found out what they were doing.

Church lawyers claim that the Powells' story is, in their words, "provable bullshit." In fact, David and the church deny any connection to the Powells. When the *Los Angeles Times* broke the story about Dwayne's following me, David's attorney said in an email to the *Times:* "Please be advised that Mr. Miscavige does not know Mr. Powell, has never heard of Mr. Powell, has never met Mr. Powell, has never spoken to Mr. Powell, never hired Mr. Powell and never directed any investigations by Mr. Powell."

Possibly one could see the point of the church's claim. After all, private investigators do not always have the best reputation. It would not have been beyond the realm of possibility that they had agreed on a story before speaking to the police in order to deflect attention from themselves and channel it onto David or the church.

If that is the angle the church is pursuing, it is not going to get it very far. The police are smart, and when there is a chance of collusion in cases such as this, they interview the parties separately without letting them confer beforehand. What's more, in this case the Powells could not have colluded because Dwayne was interrogated after being hauled down to the station, and he'd had no chance to speak to Daniel. After both had been questioned separately, the police compared the Powells' stories and they matched: They had tracked me to Aldi's market;

they saw me reach for my chest, David got on the phone shortly after Dwayne made the call and, most damning, David said, "If he dies, he dies. Don't intervene." All this was recorded by Nick Pye and the agent from the U.S. Bureau of Alcohol, Tobacco, Firearms and Explosives who participated in the questioning. I have listened to recordings of the interrogations several times. If the church wishes to back up its claim of "provable bullshit," all I can say is "good luck."

In 2014, Dwayne was indicted by a federal grand jury in Milwaukee on a firearms charge in relation to the illegal silencer. The charge against him later was dismissed after prosecutors agreed to allow him to enter a pretrial diversion program. Daniel Powell was not arrested or charged with any crime.

TWENTY-ONE

DECOMPRESSING

O N THAT EARLY AUGUST DAY, AS I SAT IN THE CONFERENCE
room at the West Allis Police Department and was briefed on the
whole matter by Nick Pye, the captain of the station came in and told
me that in all his years of police work, this was the weirdest case he had
ever known.

It was probably the weirdest thing I had ever experienced too. When
Becky and I left the church, all we wanted to do was establish a life for
ourselves. I understood that Dave would be pissed off at me because
I had left. Okay, fine, but I did not want to live that life any longer. I
wanted to restart my own life. However, I did not want to cause any
trouble for the church. My granddaughter Jenna Miscavige Hill has
written a book that explains what it was like to grow up in Scientology, *Beyond Belief: My Secret Life Inside Scientology and My Harrowing
Escape,* and it was one hell of a way to grow up. The way David treats
people and what he has done to the church are not the same as the philosophy of Scientology itself. A philosophy is just a philosophy. Nearly

everybody follows someone else's way of dealing with life or makes up their own or creates a blend of the two. Scientology was Hubbard's philosophy, and I found a lot of things in it that were helpful.

Emotionally, David's words to Dwayne over the phone shook me up a lot. I had been involved in Scientology for more than 40 years and had a high degree of certainty about what Scientology had done for me and what I had seen it do for David, my family and many others. I had seen Scientology do a lot of good for people. Yet at home later that day and in the days and weeks that followed, the foundation of my certainty developed some mighty big cracks. Hold on a minute, I thought to myself, there is something really, really wrong here. That he would have me followed and allow me to die—this guy treasures his position of wealth and power above the relationship with a father. That was hard to face.

This episode with the PIs began my search into what was really going on with Scientology. I started investigating Scientology itself and looking at L. Ron Hubbard. Up to that time, I had thought of Hubbard as more or less like a god. Here was a man who had imbued me and many others with useful knowledge about life. And that was great. I spent nearly 27 years in the Sea Org, many of which were miserable, but, because of my attitude toward life, I do not look back upon those times with a "woe is me" feeling but as simply an experience. It does not pay to play the victim. At that point, well, you are a victim.

As you can imagine, my viewpoint began to shift. I tolerated all those things in the Sea Org because I felt I was doing the best I could to help others. Many people become interested in Scientology because they have something personal they want to deal with, but when they see it working for them, they think, Hey, this is something that might help a lot of people. Let me do everything I can to help.

I began reading stuff about L. Ron Hubbard that I found on the Internet. About his marriages. About how he took ideas from other philosophers without properly crediting them. The clincher for me, though, is David's doing: today, Scientology is about strong-arming people out of their money. What the hell is this? *Fundraising?* The word has a positive connotation for charitable organizations, but in today's Church of Scientology it means "something for nothing," and that's all it means.

That really underscores why I wrote this book. I realize that by writing it I am giving up my anonymity, something I treasure. In my younger days I dreamed about being a famous musician, but as the "father of COB," I became thoroughly disabused of the idea. The church used to hold large events at the Shrine Auditorium in Los Angeles. Afterward, the crowd would congregate in an adjoining hall to buy whatever books, lecture series or courses had been released during the event. I would want to go see Becky, who would be selling, but invariably I'd be stopped every few feet by people who wanted to shake my hand and say hello. It would take me 20 minutes to make it to the far end of the hall where Becky was. Not that I was famous outside of Scientology circles, but you can imagine what it is like for famous people. You become stuck in a spot. You can't just float freely through your life. That's not for me.

Much as I cherish my anonymity today, I must do something, because the Scientology movement under David has morphed into a money-grubbing organization. No expansion has occurred that any Scientologist would recognize as such, by which I mean people being helped through auditing or by training to become auditors. Rather than concentrating on the substance of Scientology, the church today is focused merely on appearances. It just demands donations to fund fancy

TWENTY-TWO

DAVID DOES NOT GIVE UP EASILY

THINGS SETTLED DOWN AFTER THE POWELLS WERE OUT OF our lives. We moved into the house, Becky continued working and I got busy furnishing the place, selling Exer-Genies and playing gigs, mostly with Dixieland bands around Milwaukee. Nick Pye arranged for the police to keep an eye on our house in case David decided to put more PIs on me.

Ever since our escape, I had remained in regular touch with Ronnie, Denise and Lori. It was wonderful having relationships with my children and grandchildren again. They were happy to be back in contact with me. The only one not part of the picture was David. In fact, Lori and Denise, who live in Clearwater, rarely saw him in person, even though he came to town several times a year.

When Becky and I first left, my children and I talked and texted often. Later on, Lori, who I believe was acting under pressure from Dave, began insisting that Becky and I straighten out our relationship with the church after escaping the way we did. After several attempts to persuade us "to do the right thing," she finally said that she could no longer talk to us until we sorted everything out.

The church has a stupid and disgusting practice called disconnection. Other groups, such as the Jehovah's Witnesses and the Amish, have something similar, which they call shunning, but I have never heard of any group that takes it to the extremes that the Church of Scientology does.

Disconnection, in Scientology, is based on the Hubbard principle that a person should have the right to choose with whom to associate. If someone is continually bothering you, you should have the right to not communicate with the bothersome source. That makes sense. Society has mechanisms such as restraining orders to take care of this. The justice system "disconnects" people by sticking them in prison. No one will argue against the necessity of disconnection on occasion. The Church of Scientology, however, perverts that concept to the point of breaking up and destroying families, ruining people's businesses and even their lives. And for what? For things as simple as criticizing the church or disagreeing with its tactics or wanting to leave the group.

The church will say that disconnection is not a required practice in the church, but saying that relies on a fundamentally dishonest logic. Here is the "logic" behind the lie: If a Scientologist does something that the church doesn't like, such as criticizing it, the church will hit back by declaring the person an enemy and labeling that individual a "suppressive person." This means that the person is out to squash or suppress anyone who is trying to better themselves or to suppress any group that tries to help people, in other words, first and foremost, the Church of Scientology. Accordingly, any Scientologist who remains in contact with someone who has been labeled suppressive is guilty by association and therefore must be barred from receiving any further services from the church. "So," church representatives will say, "it's your own free choice whether you choose to remain in communication with Joe Blow." Of course, if you choose *not* to cut your family member out of your life, you will no longer be able to participate in Scientology. Oh, and any other Scientologists you know will be given the same choice in regard to *you*. This will likely include your friends, family members, associates and, often, your employer. Do you want to keep your job, your friends, family and your continued progress in Scientology, or do you want to keep talking to that no good son of yours who had the nerve to speak his mind about Scientology? You're free to make your own decision!

That is a little background on disconnection, and why Lori decided to stop communicating with me. Being the father of the leader of the church has not exempted me from being affected by disconnection. Some months later, Denise also succumbed to the pressure, and she disconnected from me as well. Ronnie, who had left Scientology more than a decade before I did, was no longer willing to play that game, and, bless him, we talk and visit often.

Philosophically, the idea of disconnection flies in the face of *the* single most important of the fundamental principles of Scientology, which is that communication is the universal solution and that more communication, not less, is the path to resolving *any* issue. So Becky and I decided that we would plant ourselves on Lori's and Denise's doorsteps and see if communication could change their determination to cut us out of their lives. Bear in mind that we continued to receive occasional text messages from Denise but no letters or emails or phone calls. Those ceased in late summer 2013, right around the time that the Powells were busted.

Becky worked out a plan to keep a channel to the family open. In October 2013, a friend of hers was moving to Florida and Becky agreed to make the trip down with her. Becky's idea was to try to re-establish some sort of communication with Denise and other family members when she and her friend stopped in Clearwater. Becky was not able to contact Denise but did reestablish relationships with Denise's ex-husband and one of Denise's daughters. During the next year, we sent letters to Denise and learned that when her daughter asked about the letters, Denise often broke down in tears and said, "We can't talk about that. Don't pressure me. Don't ask me about them anymore." Yet the Church of Scientology claims that disconnection is not mandatory!

The next year was calm for Becky and me. We did not think we were still being followed, but a particularly strange episode occurred in September 2014.

Our normal garbage pickup day is Wednesday. The pickup schedule got pushed back because of the Monday Labor Day holiday. We put the garbage out on Tuesday evenings as always, because we did not realize the schedule had changed. All day Wednesday the garbage stayed out on the curb. On Thursday, before the rescheduled pickup, Becky noticed a bag of garbage sitting out in the street, and it looked like one of the bags we ordinarily used, so she went outside to retrieve it and put it in the can. When she opened the lid, she saw that the bag had indeed been removed from our can and that lying on top of the remaining bags was a dead rat that I had killed earlier and dropped in the garbage. Someone had been rifling through our garbage, pulled the top bag out, saw the rat and vamoosed. When Becky checked the bag, it confirmed her suspicions that someone had been looking through our trash. This is a typical ploy used by the church to gain information about someone they are following. We later learned that Nick Pye also had his garbage stolen on a couple occasions right around that time.

In October, Becky and I drove down to Clearwater to try to resolve the family impasse once and for all. A week before we left, Denise's daughter texted us to say, "My mom knows you're coming." We still have no idea how she knew, though Nick Pye tells me that some of our friends are informants for the church. Still, we had every hope that my daughters would consent to talk to us so we could resolve the roadblock that the church had erected in our relationship. We did not think that the church was still having us followed, but the message from Denise's daughter raised our suspicions.

Unbeknown to us, another player would enter the drama that was about to unfold. I have been friends with Lisa Marie Presley for a long time. We first met at the maiden voyage of the *Freewinds* cruise ship in 1988. That first voyage was a big deal in the world of Scientology, and the ship was packed with important Scientologists and Scientology celebrities. Lisa Marie and I somehow were introduced to each other and hit it off. We spent a lot of time chatting in the ship's lounge during the cruise. Over the years, she came to the Gold base occasionally, and she and I used those opportunities to renew our friendship. After Becky and I left in 2012, I contacted Lisa Marie, and we have remained in close touch since. We talk on the phone often, and she and I were catching up on the latest when I told her that Becky and I were driving down to Florida.

"Ron, you're never going to guess where I am right now."

"I have no idea. Memphis? We're in Tennessee right now."

"I'm near Clearwater. I'm here taking care of some things for the next few days."

"CW? Get out of here! We'll be in town tomorrow!"

We promised to talk again and get together if the opportunity presented itself.

We made it to Clearwater, and on the first day we went to both Lori's and Denise's houses. Lori was not home. At Denise's, we spoke to her husband for 20 minutes through a crack in the door, but he never did allow us to see Denise.

The conversation went nowhere. Finally, at the end I said, "Okay, Jerry, let me put it to you straight: Does this mean that you and Denise are through with us forever?"

"Yes, Ron, we are through with you and Becky forever."

If I ever had misgivings about telling the world my story and about my son David, those vanished right there on Denise's doorstep. At that moment I decided to write this book.

We left and went back to Lori's place. Her car was out front, so we knocked on the door for several minutes but she would not answer. That ended our first day, and I would not call it a success.

On our second day, we drove about an hour south of Clearwater to have brunch with an old friend from our days at Gold. A mile from where we were staying, Becky noticed a black Jeep that seemed to be following us. She drove for another 20 miles before telling me what was going on. She wanted to be certain. Our earlier suspicions were confirmed. We were again being followed by private investigators. Three of them, in separate vehicles. After brunch, we drove back to Clearwater and were followed again. Nick Pye and the West Allis Police Department ran their plates, so we knew who the PIs were; still, it was distressing.

What I did not know at the time was that Lisa Marie had decided to see if she could help me reconnect with my daughters. She and David had been friends at one time, and she thought that perhaps she could help. She went into the church's headquarters in downtown Clearwater and spoke to David's representatives. Later, she told me what happened. She was livid at the prospect of my not being able to talk to my daughters and the hypocrisy of the church's claim that it has no policy of disconnection, yet clearly it was affecting the family of the Chairman of the Board! There are cameras in the Religious Technology Center offices in Clearwater, and Lisa said that she wanted to deliver a message directly to David, so she spoke directly to the cameras. From what she told me later, she let him have it pretty good. "How dare you not let your own father talk to his daughters? You are breaking up the family!" Irony of ironies, the church was in the process of holding a Family Day public relations event extolling the values of family life and showing its support for all families everywhere.

A couple of days later, Lisa Marie received an astonishing response to her remarks. She and her husband were back in the Religious Technology Center office. Church officials apparently had decided that since Lisa Marie was concerned about my family, they were going to let my daughters address the problem. The message from the church was, basically, "Since you care so much about families, we want you to hear what Denise and Lori have to say." What Lisa Marie relayed to me afterward was that the whole thing felt staged for her benefit. As if on cue, Denise and Lori came into the office. They had obviously been briefed and were stirred up and ready to kill.

Denise lashed out at Lisa Marie and stomped around like David does, cursing and gesticulating and slamming her fist on the desk. She fulminated about how I had hit Loretta and how I did this and how I did that, yelling that she, Denise, never wanted anything to do with me again. Apparently, it was quite a performance. Lisa Marie's husband told me afterward that watching Denise do her thing was like seeing Dave with a wig on blowing a gasket.

In all probability, the cameras were on so the scene could be replayed for David, if he wasn't sitting somewhere watching it in real time. David had helped Denise when she had a scrape with the law in 2013, something that has been written about elsewhere, so basically she now feels beholden to him, in my opinion. In other words, her performance was for her twin brother more than it was to make a point with Lisa Marie.

Denise had seen all the arguments and fights between Loretta and me over the years, and that had never stopped her from being in contact with me. Now, all of a sudden, that is a deal breaker? Who's kidding whom? Denise witnessed, grew up with and lived with the strife that Loretta and I had in our marriage. Now, fifty years later, when Becky and I are trying to resolve our relationship with Denise, not Loretta, what happened in the 1960s suddenly makes reconciliation impossible? Some people evidently think that if they can yell loud enough, the illogic of their arguments will pass unnoticed.

Yet, just a few years earlier, Denise and Lori had made a special point to come all the way to Los Angeles to spend time with me. They had been asking for me to come to Florida for a visit, but I was never able to get away. They decided, that's it; we're coming to see you. David was in Clearwater at the time, and Lori went to see him in his office. Since I was never able to get back east to see them, she told David that she and Denise wanted to come out to visit me. He relented and they flew to Los Angeles. Odd that a daughter would have to check with her brother before visiting with her father, isn't it? That is Scientology today under David. Denise and Lori stayed at Scientology's Celebrity Centre International hotel in Hollywood, and I was able to go down to see them. We spent four really good days together, talking, eating good food, relaxing and basically just being a family. We all thoroughly enjoyed it. Not only that, but in 2012 they sent me 75 gifts for my seventy-fifth birthday. Each year, for my birthday and Father's Day as well as Christmas, they always sent me beautiful gifts. There had always been a lot of love between us. Whenever I took a leave in the early years, I went to visit them and we had terrific times together. And now Denise won't talk to me because Loretta and I used to fight? Is there anyone alive who believes this is sincere?

You can imagine the impression the entire show made on Lisa Marie and her husband. If these insanities are occurring with immediate family members of the leader of the entire church, what else must be going on with other families throughout Scientology?

For the rest of our visit to Clearwater, we stayed with Bobby Covington, Denise's ex-husband. Bobby's wife and their kids found the ensuing cat-and-mouse games we played with the PIs exciting, and the games continued until we left town. We were followed the entire time.

Two weeks later, I began writing my story.

TWENTY-THREE

THE CON THAT IS SCIENTOLOGY TODAY

THE CATHOLIC CHURCH HAD A TEACHING KNOWN AS INDUL-
gences. A sinner could receive a pardon for sins by confessing them
and then doing good works, saying prayers and things of that nature.
Indulgences were church doctrine even in its early days. By the late
Middle Ages some marketing genius in the Vatican hit on the idea of
dispensing with the prayers and good works and simply selling an in-
dulgence for money.

In my mind, this describes perfectly the state of the Church of Scientology today. In earlier years, the organization obtained its wherewithal
by charging Scientologists for the services of auditing and training and
by selling the materials used in training, such as books and lectures.
Scientologists considered these services valuable and were willing to exchange money for them. Since the early 2000s though, the emphasis has
shifted to asking Scientologists to donate money for different projects

in exchange for a pat on the back. In other words, something for nothing. David Miscavige has been selling Scientologists a bill of goods, and
the con goes like this: In the past, Scientology's buildings were often
rundown and did not present a good public image. The first Scientology structure to draw David's attention was in Buffalo, where the city
planned to invoke eminent domain and take the church building, which
lay in the path of a public works project. Around the same time, the
world's most famous Scientologist, Tom Cruise, complained to David
that he could not take a person he was trying to interest in Scientology
into a local church because it looked so bad, or so I have been told. These
events spurred David to come up with a program that is meant to turn
every Scientology church into an "ideal" organization. The operation
involves buying a building in a city and then renovating it to make it utterly posh, which, the logic goes, will attract people to Scientology.

To fund the extensive costs for these "ideal orgs," David, through
his minions, persuades public Scientologists to donate millions for the
purchase of the building and then millions more to pay for the renovations. This might be excusable if the building then was solely for the
benefit of the local area. This is not how David works, however. From
his position, he dictates everything of importance that happens in the
church, which means he controls those considerable real estate assets as
well. Although owned by the local church, the new "ideal org" comes
under the management of the Landlord Office at International Management headquarters, which puts it directly under David's control. It
makes Scientology look bigger and, on the surface, as though Scientology is expanding. My son is nothing if not clever.

Making my point even more strongly is that many services once
delivered regularly in Scientology organizations are no longer available. Volumes and volumes containing all of Hubbard's organizational
policies were once for sale. These are no longer available on the church

websites that publish Scientology materials. An advanced auditor training course involves studying of all Hubbard's books, all of his bulletins relating to auditing theory and procedures, and hundreds of his
lectures. This massive course takes at least a year of full-time study,
and the course has been a mainstay service for Scientologists since the
1960s when Hubbard inaugurated it. That course is no longer available, according to reports about the Los Angeles organization, which
delivered it for decades. Other courses that thousands of Scientologists
had taken for decades appear to be in a similar category. None of those
course materials are available for sale on church websites. Excuses are
given for their withdrawal, but apparently it is far easier and less work to
harangue Scientologists for straight donations than to actually deliver
services to them that take weeks or months.

A good friend of mine, Dave Richards, once compared Scientology
in its heyday to what it is today. Richards knew about this comparison
because for several years he was the director of the Founding Church
of Scientology in Washington, D.C. Hubbard was always keen on mea-
suring how productive every church organization was, and the church
kept weekly production statistics. Richards told me that when he was
running the church, it delivered 1,200 hours of auditing every week,
enough to keep 50 auditors busy; today those figures may well match
the entire amount delivered by the 150 or so midlevel churches all over
the world. The Washington church regularly had 200 people in training to become auditors, and upward of 50 each week were coming in
for introductory courses. For years Mike Rinder has published on his
popular blog photos taken by former Scientologists of churches in various cities, and they are largely empty, not only of parishioners but of
staff too!

Predictably, the "ideal org" strategy has backfired for everyone but
David himself. The parishioners in the local organization drained their

bank accounts, maxed out their credit cards, spent their children's college savings, took out second mortgages and otherwise accepted financial strain. The staff of the local organization, which ordinarily had difficulty paying the bills, now has much larger heating, air-conditioning and electricity bills. The new church is large and beautiful but stands mostly empty of people because the parishioners have been pressured into using their discretionary income and much more to put the building there in the first place.

David, however, has made out like a bandit, and I use the term advisedly.

Each new "ideal org" adds millions in value to the coffers of Scientology International. The most important performance indicator of Scientology's management is called Sea Org Reserves (SOR), which is the amount of wealth in money, property, whatever, that the church has saved up. According to Mike Rinder, the value of these new church buildings is added to the SOR statistic periodically, and doing so paints a rosy picture for management. David micromanages nearly every aspect of Scientology operations, and certainly every important one, and you can be sure that these new buildings in the Scientology real estate portfolio are some of his biggest chips.

David's position of absolute authority in the church brings to mind the analogy of a military strongman who lives a lavish lifestyle while the citizens of the country live in poverty. David has well-appointed apartments or living facilities in all of Scientology's major centers: the headquarters in Hemet, Los Angeles, Clearwater, St. Hill in England and aboard the *Freewinds*. As I have mentioned, he has only the highest quality food served at every meal. At the Hemet base, he had an exercise facility built that only he and certain celebrities such as Tom Cruise are allowed to use. Incidentally, because of my lifelong interest in exercise, I researched, found and bought the equipment for the gym. The church furnishes all his vehicles and transportation, including motorcycles, cars and vans. He wears suits tailored by top Los Angeles tailors and once received a $10,000 suit from one for his birthday. And speaking of birthdays, every April the churches around the world pressure their meagerly paid staff to buy birthday presents for him. Rank-and-file Sea Org members receive a standard allowance of $50 a week for incidentals. Many weeks, however, this amount is reduced because of financial pressures, sometimes to zero. During some years we were paid nothing throughout most of the year—except when it was time to shell out for David's Christmas or birthday presents. Still, after the weekly staff meeting at which everyone lines up to collect their pay, someone is there to take 30 or 40 percent of their pittance to help buy COB a new camera or high-end mountain bike or high-tech gadget. The same thing happens at Christmas when different organizations try to outdo one another to express their gratitude. Make no mistake: David's position of absolute power is a comfortable and well-feathered nest.

I recall a time when he walked in wearing a nice pair of shoes. "I got the shoes I told you about while I was over in England," he said. "Custom made."

"Good-looking shoes," I said. "How much did they cost?"

"Fifteen hundred bucks."

I was stunned. Fifteen hundred dollars is what I made in the Sea Org for an entire year's work. At that time, Sea Org members made $30 a week. Yet he had the wherewithal to drop $1,500 on a single pair of shoes.

David obviously saw the look on my face and told me in a somewhat embarrassed tone, "You know, these really do feel different," trying to convince me that these nice shoes really were worth ten or more times the usual price of a decent pair.

All the booty David accumulates doesn't take a dime out of his pocket. Sea Org members are meant to be rewarded for their production. What they produce on their jobs is counted up weekly, and Hubbard recommended that, for stellar performance, staff should receive bonuses on top of their allowance. Dave has worked it out so that he receives not only weekly bonuses but also hefty year-end bonuses. The allowance that other Sea Org members receive isn't even an afterthought for him. A former RTC staff member who worked in its finance division told me that David would have shirts custom made at a cost of $200 each, and he would wear them *once*. Maybe this was for special events but still. Once? Scientology is supposed to be a church.

In comparison, other Sea Org members live like monks. Their weekly allowance would not pay for activities on a day off, if they were ever allowed a day off. I have already mentioned the difference in the food allowance. As for living quarters, unmarried men and women live in dorms for each, while married couples have single rooms. Quarters are not lavish by any means. Sea Org members are furnished with uniforms, but when items wear out, people are expected to buy replacements out of pocket. You can bet that church public relations executives will counter what I write by showing the beautiful facilities at the Gold base—the soccer fields, basketball and tennis courts, running path with exercise stations, the nine-hole golf course, Olympic-size swimming pool, the landscaping with manicured lawns and tended flower beds and functional but beautiful architecture. And they would be right: the facilities at Gold are first rate. Of course, staff members work in the production spaces for as long as 24 hours a day and rarely, if ever, get to enjoy the recreational facilities. At one time L. Ron Hubbard mandated that all staff should have one hour a day for exercise. It was to be in the daily schedule, he ordered. And at times, the staff was allowed this time. It would be implemented, and people would begin exercising. Two weeks later, some emergency, or "flap," would happen and exercise time would drop out again, only to be resurrected some years later, again for a week or two. While David lives like a prince wherever he travels and flies first class or in Tom Cruise's private jet, the rest of the Sea Org lives like indentured servants, at best.

To be truthful, though, I would not begrudge him any of the perks of his leadership if he had remained true to the humanitarian objectives laid out by L. Ron Hubbard. Instead, David has managed to do virtually the opposite, for purposes, it seems, of keeping himself and a handful of well-paid lawyers living comfortable lifestyles.

I write all this to make what I think is the central point of my story: there is a world of difference between what I found workable in the actual philosophy of Scientology and how David has twisted it to his own ends. How did it come to this? How did a young boy who was an affectionate, happy, bright kid with a great sense of humor and a desire to help others grow into a man who surrounds himself only with people who suck up to him and lives a lavish lifestyle while those who work for him live no better than medieval serfs? What is the catalyst for such an unfortunate transformation?

I have concluded that it is the acquisition of power. Some who come into positions of power may be able to remain whole and true to themselves, but my son David has demonstrated beyond doubt that he is not one of them.

TWENTY-FOUR

NOW WHAT?

THE DEGREE TO WHICH DAVID HAS DEVIATED FROM L. RON
Hubbard's management directives since he took power in the
1980s has had several consequences that I don't think he ever predicted.
The most significant of these, in my opinion, is the appearance of more
and more people still practicing Scientology but entirely outside the
church's control. The phenomenon of Scientologists' splintering away
from the organization occurred even in its early days as people here and
there fell into disfavor with Hubbard or vice versa and went off on their
own. In the early 1980s, though, the first major schism in church history took place, and David was at the center of it.

The smaller Scientology organizations are called missions. They
deliver basic entry-level courses and auditing and act as a feeder line
to churches. Historically, there was always some tension between the
missions and the full-fledged churches because missions were under
looser control, they could pay their staff better and so forth. Often, the
better, more highly trained auditors would opt to work for a mission,

where the pay was better, instead of at a church. When David gained the position as Hubbard's gatekeeper, he stoked Hubbard's ire at the mission network as a whole. Finally, Hubbard ordered wholesale actions to curb what he thought were the excesses of the mission holders (the people who owned and ran their missions) and their continual stealing of parishioners from the churches. David and his henchmen were only too happy to flex their Sea Org muscle and oblige Hubbard's demands.

In 1982, David and his henchmen held meetings in San Francisco and elsewhere. According to published accounts, they gathered mission holders in a room and read them the riot act. Certain mission holders were declared suppressive persons on the spot, for the purpose of cowing the rest into submission. Missions were now going to come under church control, and their use of the church's trademarks would be strictly regulated. The result of this ham-fisted approach was destruction of the mission network, a purge of the most successful mission holders, a drastic increase in financial demands by the church, and the end of feeder lines into churches, which only put more stress on them. Shock waves went through the entire Scientology network, and the mission network has never recovered.

Some people, now thoroughly disaffected with management and the organization but still loyal to the principles and practice of Scientology, simply set up shop outside the auspices of the church and continued to deliver Scientology but at greatly reduced rates. The church now had a kind of free-market competition.

One of the people who began operating in what was called the Freezone was David Mayo, the auditor who helped Hubbard recover from the severe illness he suffered in 1978 and who held the highest technical position in Scientology for a number of years. In 1982, Mayo fell into disfavor with David and Pat Broeker, based, so far as I know, on the idea that Mayo was antimanagement for his objections to high prices for services, what he considered financial waste at the Gold base, and for injustices he saw happening at the time. Within a year he was no longer in the Sea Org. Still seeing value in the practice of Scientology, however, Mayo set up shop near Santa Barbara and began delivering Scientology auditing. Loretta and I seriously considered going to his group because the church donation rates were spiraling out of control. Scientology was no longer affordable for the average working person and, increasingly, became limited only to the wealthy. We didn't go to Santa Barbara, but only because of David's position at the top of the Sea Org.

Since that first major splintering, many more people have left the church but continue to practice Scientology. Today there are independent practitioners in virtually every part of the world where Scientology has adherents. In Israel, an entire mission broke from the church and now delivers the entirety of Scientology services to a growing number of Scientologists. A whole network of organizations that espouse Hubbard's methodologies exists, primarily in Europe, and it has no association with the Church of Scientology. The church is either powerless, or unwilling, to stop them. Any intellectual property arguments the church might be tempted to pursue against people using the ideas and philosophical underpinnings of Scientology outside the church would not go far, I think, particularly in light of recent studies of mine, which demonstrate that many ideas Hubbard claimed for *Dianetics* and Scientology apparently came from earlier sources.

A couple years ago a friend introduced me to the writers of the New Thought movement, which I mentioned earlier. Numerous books written 50 or more years before Hubbard developed *Dianetics* contain many of the same elements that Hubbard incorporated in his work, whether he was aware of these sources or not. One is *How to Heal Oneself and Others: Mental Therapeutics,* written in 1918 by William Walker Atkinson under the pen name Theron Q. Dumont. Atkinson was a tremendously prolific writer who turned out 100 books during the last 30 years of his life. *How to Heal Oneself* offers an explanation of the subconscious mind that appears in *Dianetics* and Scientology as the *reactive mind*. This is the mind that never sleeps and records everything that happens to a person. Atkinson's book also contains the procedure that became known in Scientology as solo auditing, wherein a person serves both as the counselor and counselee.

Charles F. Haanel's *The Master Key System*, written at the turn of the twentieth century, contains in its first lesson an almost exact description of the basic communication training drill practiced in Scientology for more than 40 years. Another book is *The Law of Psychic Phenomena* by Thomson Jay Hudson. Then there is *Working with the Law* by Raymond Holliwell. Anyone can find these books and many more through a simple search of the New Thought movement writers; many are available for free on the Internet.

I'm not discounting the fact that L. Ron Hubbard may have made worthwhile discoveries of his own that do not appear in these earlier works or anywhere else that I know of. But it bears repeating that many fundamentals about the mind and life can be found outside Scientology. The point, I think, is to find something that works for you and use that and discard things that don't. Maybe it takes a touch of humility to consider that perhaps you could learn more about yourself and your life. I understand and accept that many people will not even consider my words because Scientology has such a bad odor generally. I don't deny that the reputation is well deserved. At the same time, I can't help but equate that bias with the attitudes that early Christians held about Rome. Anything and everything about Rome was to be detested; so, because the Romans bathed, the practice of bathing went out the window for God knows how long.

Another point I want to make is that, regardless of what L. Ron Hubbard did in his personal life, Scientology makes available common-sense ideas that people can use on their own, without having to be connected to an organization or pledge allegiance to some cult or grand poobah or burn through their life savings or break up their families. Hubbard codified a great many notions that many people have found useful, and all of it is more or less freely available.

Someone once asked me what I think should be done with the church. I have seen Scientology at all levels, from Frank Ogle's Keystone Kops Tuesday evening meetings in a café to its international headquarters in California and every place in between. I have known Scientology from when it was a comparatively footloose and fancy-free association of people having fun and finding things out about themselves to the controlling East Germany–under-the-Stasi cult it is today. I have studied Scientology thoroughly and in depth and have had personal subjective experiences that I would term miracles, so I know there is value in Hubbard's work. I also know that many of the same principles exist in other places without the organizational baggage that comes with joining a Scientology organization, as currently constituted under my son David. For these and other reasons, I think I am qualified to offer an opinion.

I could propose many reforms, but three stand out. First, the disgraceful practice of disconnection should be abandoned completely and utterly. This is the poison that Scientology throws into its own well on a daily basis. Making people disconnect from their loved ones or making their loved ones disconnect from them is unconscionable any way you slice it. This practice affects me, even to this day. It must cease.

My next reform would be to grant a general amnesty and forgive everybody who ran afoul of the church for whatever reason. With no strings attached. Just a straight "You are forgiven." This, of course, might have some repercussions for church order. Hubbard said that when you attempt to straighten out a disordered area, things usually get a little messier before they become more orderly. The church would have to be ready to face those repercussions, but in the long run forgiveness would soothe many troubled waters.

The final reform would be to knock off the obsession with shaking down Scientologists for money to fund new buildings that they don't need. Start offering simple services that people can afford, and that will help them improve their lives.

I don't say that this is all that needs to be done to reform Scientology or that it might not still be riddled with bad policies if these three restructurings were enacted. Still, in my mind, these are the greatest wrongs that I see Scientology inflicting on itself and anyone connected with it.

Will any of these ideas be implemented so long as David remains in control? Not on your life. Still, one can always hope and dream. When you stop dreaming, you die a little, a wise man once said.

Is there enough of value in Scientology to make it even worth salvaging? Only time will tell, but so long as David remains in charge, it is a moot point.

A FINAL WORD

THERE IS SO MUCH HATE IN THE WORLD THAT EVERYBODY could take a second helping. Nelson Mandela spoke the God's honest truth when he said that holding on to anger is like drinking poison and hoping the other person dies. I have no interest in adding to the amount of hate and anger in the world. I am simply not going to be part of it.

I once knew of two sisters who did not speak to one another for 20 years. Yet they lived next door to each other. They would be out back, hanging their laundry on the line and looking the other way, never saying a word. I don't view that as a criticism of them so much as it is a criticism of the way people sometimes think. More communication, not less, is the way to move beyond a dispute or upset. True, the shit may hit the fan, but if you keep on talking, you *will* sort it out.

The disconnection policy that the church follows resolves nothing because it stops any communication. "Someone had critical thoughts about us, disconnect from him. Okay, that's handled," or so goes the logic. That only exacerbates the situation. That only makes it worse for the countless people who are disconnected from their families. Through this policy the church sows seeds of discontent and harvests the results.

Here I am, the father of the leader of the Church of Scientology, and I'm writing a book. What do you think of that? Left to my own devices, all I wanted to do was sell Exer-Genies, play my horn, maybe write some more humorous books about the characters I have met, and enjoy life.

In the final analysis, after all that went down with David's ordering people to follow me for a year, telling Dwayne Powell that if I was having a heart attack to let me die, the policy of disconnection that means my daughters and most of their children will not talk to me, and all the rest of it, I will say only this: David, I think you have made mistakes and, from my viewpoint, serious ones.

But what I also want to say—and this has nothing to do with my trying to look like a good guy or elicit approval from anyone reading this, but only with my belief that it is the only way for me to move forward—that I hope things will change someday. But for now, and I mean this from the bottom of my heart:

David, I forgive you.

ACKNOWLEDGMENTS

I want to thank some of the people who have supported me throughout the process of writing this book and telling my story. Their help has made the job a lot easier for me and more informative than it would have been otherwise, and I appreciate them very much.

First and foremost is my wonderful wife, Becky, who has been with me for the past 25 years of my journey and has made all the difference in my life.

To my son Ronnie; Dave Richards, a longtime friend; Detective Nick Pye of the West Allis Police Department; John Peterson of Transformetrics, who introduced me to *The Master Key System;* and especially to my collaborator, Dan Koon, thank you very, very much.

I also want to acknowledge a list of people who gave me their support, their feedback and their advice throughout the process of telling my story. Many of the following supplied me with information, corroborated my own recollections and otherwise helped me share a more complete picture of my son David. These friends and acquaintances include Mike Rinder; Terri and Fernando Gamboa; Marc and Claire Headley; Steve Hall; Gale Irwin; Mark Fisher; Nori Matsamaru; Betsy Stieg; Lisa Marie Presley; my agents, Jane Dystel and Miriam Goderich; and my editor at St. Martin's, Karen Wolny. Thank you, one and all.

SUGGESTED READING

Some readers may have had their curiosity piqued by my mention in my story of certain authors and their works. Following is a list of books that I think may satisfy that interest, some by L. Ron Hubbard, others by writers who were part of the New Thought movement. The Scientology books by Hubbard are pretty fundamental and don't contain any of the organizational concepts that I feel have made the church so reviled. Any of the following titles can be found online, either for free or at low cost, and contain, in my opinion, some valuable information:

L. Ron Hubbard, *Self Analysis*
L. Ron Hubbard, *A New Slant on Life*
L. Ron Hubbard, *The Fundamentals of Thought*
William Walker Atkinson (writing as Theron Q. Dumont), *How to Heal Oneself and Others: Mental Therapeutics*
Charles F. Haanel, *The Master Key System*
Prentice Mulford, *The Prentice Mulford Collection*
R. H. Jarrett, *It Works*